Dedication

This book is for those who risk their lives every day to keep the streets drug free. God bless and keep up the good work.

Authors Note

The views and events expressed in this book are for educational and/or entertainment purposes only. I in no way condone or agree with drug trafficking/trade and, in-fact, have spent many years fighting it. If you are stupid enough to believe you can profit in this illegal trade, I have included the instructions listed in the "everybody profits" chapter. Furthermore, I have included information on commonplace drugs as I believe that everyone should be well informed of the "product" available. While the title indicates that the book will be humorous throughout, drug use and trafficking is no laughing matter. Therefore, the humor has been left for the end of the book.

Thank You.

Semi-Famous Quotes About Drugs

"I tried marijuana once. I did not inhale" - Former President Bill Clinton

"Drugs are a waste of time. They Destroy your memory and your self-respect and everything that goes along with your self-esteem." - Kurt Cobain

"Today's students can put dope in their veins or hope in their brains. If they can conceive it and believe it, they can achieve it. They must know it is not their aptitude but their attitude that will determine their altitude." - Rev. Jessie Jackson

"Herb is the healing of a nation, alcohol is the destruction." - Bob Marley

"Dope never helped anybody sing better or play music better or do anything better. All dope can do for you is kill you – and kill you the long, slow, hard way." Billie Holiday

"The sixties were when hallucinogenic drugs were really, really big. And I don't think it's a coincidence that we had the type of shows we had then, like The Flying Nun." - Ellen DeGeneres

"The best pitch I ever heard about was back in the early eighties when a street dealer followed me down the sidewalk going: I got some great blow man. I got the stuff that killed Belushi." - Denis Leary

"Ah, pierce me 100 times with your needles fine and I will thank you 100 times, St. Morphine, you who Asclepius has made a God." - Jules Verne

"Don't do drugs because if you do drugs you'll go to prison, and drugs are really expensive in prison." - John Hardwick

"Drugs have taught an entire generation of American kids the metric system." - P.J. O'Rourke

"I tried sniffing coke once, but the ice cubes got stuck in my nose." Author Unknown

"Thou hast the keys of Paradise, oh, just, subtle, and mighty opium!" - Thomas De Quincey, from Confessions of an English Opium-Eater, Part III

"Cocaine is God's way of saying you're making too much money." - Robin Williams

"Drugs are very much a part of professional sports today, but when you think about it, golf is the only sport where the players aren't penalized for being on grass." - Bob Hope

"I don't intend for this to take on a political tone. I'm just here for the drugs." - Nancy Reagan

"Do you think God gets stoned? I think so...look at the platypus." Robin Williams

An Overview of the Illegal Drug Trade

The illegal drug trade is a global black market consisting of the cultivation, manufacture, distribution and sale of illegal controlled drugs. Most jurisdictions prohibit trade, except under license, of many types of drugs by drug control laws. Some drugs, notably alcohol and tobacco, are outside the scope of these laws, but may be subject to control under other laws.

The illicit drug trade operates similarly to other underground markets. Various drug cartels specialize in the separate processes along the supply chain, often localized to maximize production efficiency and minimize damages caused by law enforcement. Depending on the profitability of each layer, cartels usually vary in size, consistency, and organization. The chain ranges from low-level street dealers who may be individual drug users themselves, through street gangs and contractor-like middle men, up to multinational empires that rival governments in size.

Illegal drugs may be grown in wilderness areas, on farms, produced in indoor/outdoor residential gardens, indoor hydroponics grow-ops, or manufactured in drug labs located anywhere from a residential basement to an abandoned facility. The common characteristic binding these production locations is that they are discreet to avoid other black marketeers. Corruption is a large problem, especially in the poorer societies.

Consumption of illegal drugs is widespread globally. While consumers avoid taxation by buying on the black market, the high costs involved in protecting trade routes from law often lead to inflated prices.

Additionally, various laws criminalize certain kinds of trade of drugs that are otherwise legal (for example, untaxed cigarettes). In these cases, the drugs are often manufactured and partially distributed by the normal legal channels, and diverted at some point into illegal channels.

Finally, many governments restrict the production and sale of large classes of drugs through prescription systems.

* * *

The trade of drugs has existed for as long as drugs themselves have existed. However, the trade of drugs was fully legal until the introduction of drug prohibition. The history of the illegal drug trade is thus closely tied to the history of drug prohibition. In the First Opium War, the United Kingdom forced China to allow British merchants to trade in opium with the general population of China. Although illegal by imperial decree, smoking opium had become common in the 1800s due to increasing importation via British merchants. Trading in opium was extremely lucrative. As a result of the trade an estimated two million Chinese people became addicted to the drug. The British Crown took vast sums of money from the Chinese government in what they referred to as 'reparations' for the wars.

Mafia groups limited their activities to gambling and theft until 1920, when organized bootlegging manifested in response to the effect of Prohibition. An example of the spectacular rise of the mafia due to Prohibition is Al Capone's syndicate that "ruled" Chicago in the 1920s.

Some governments that criminalize drug trade have a policy of interfering heavily with foreign states. In 1989, the United States intervened in Panama with the goal of disrupting the drug trade coming from Panama. The Indian government has several covert operations in the Middle East and Indian subcontinent to keep a track of various drug dealers. Opium production in Afghanistan is a current impediment in the development of an illicit economy for that country.

* * *

The U.S. Federal Government is a vocal opponent of the drug industry, however state laws vary greatly and in some cases defy federal laws. Despite the US government's official position against the drug trade, US government agents and assets have been implicated in the drug trade and were caught and investigated during the Iran-Contra scandal, implicated in the use of the drug trade as a secret source of funding for the USA's support of the Contras. Page 41 of the December 1988 Kerry report to the US Senate states that "indeed senior US policy makers were not immune to the idea that drug money was a perfect solution to the Contra's funding problem".

Highly decorated retired US military Special Forces veteran Colonel Bo Gritz has accused the USA of collaborating with and supporting Manuel Noriega in his drug trafficking operations. In his book Called To Serve,

Gritz details his role as a key US Government employee tasked with protecting the USA's relationship with Noriega.

Contrary to its official goals, the US has suppressed research on drug usage. For example, in 1995 the World Health Organization (WHO) and the United Nations Inter-regional Crime and Justice Research Institute (UNICRI) announced in a press release the publication of the results of the largest global study on cocaine use ever undertaken. However, a decision in the World Health Assembly banned the publication of the study. In the sixth meeting of the B committee the US House of Representatives threatened that "If WHO activities relating to drugs failed to reinforce proven drug control approaches, funds for the relevant programs should be curtailed". This led to the decision to discontinue publication.

* * *

Most of the effects of the illegal drug trade are not unique to the drug trade -- they are endemic and to be expected with any black market and should be expected to worsen with increased efforts to eliminate the market with no decrease in demand. The countries of drug production, which are usually developing countries, have been seen as the worst affected by global drug trade. The youth of countries like Afghanistan, Kazakhstan, Tajikistan, where drugs like heroin are produced, see drugs as a point of contact with the West. To them the use of drugs represents modernity and is associated with the glitz and glam of developed nations, such as fancy cars and big houses. The drugs are seen as a doorway to a better life; while in reality drugs produce long term consequences and problems in societies, such as health problems (like the spread of HIV/AIDS), and further socio-economic and political instability.

The U.S. government's most recent 2005 National Survey on Drug Use and Health (NSDUH) reported that nationwide over 800,000 adolescents ages 12-17 sold illegal drugs during the twelve months preceding the survey; such adolescents also admitted to know or be linked to other drug dealers across the nation. The 2005 Youth Risk Behavior Survey by the U.S. Centers for Disease Control and Prevention (CDC) reported that nationwide 25.4% of students had been offered, sold, or given an illegal drug by someone on school property. The prevalence of having been offered, sold, or given an illegal drug on school property ranged from 15.5% to 38.7% across state CDC surveys (median: 26.1%) and from 20.3% to 40.0% across local surveys (median: 29.4%).

Despite over $7 billion spent annually towards arresting and prosecuting nearly 800,000 people across the country for marijuana offenses in 2005 (FBI Uniform Crime Reports), the federally-funded Monitoring the Future

Survey reports about 85% of high school seniors find marijuana "easy to obtain." That figure has remained virtually unchanged since 1975, never dropping below 82.7% in three decades of national surveys.

Unfortunately drug abuse often affects the youth turning a source of vibrant productivity into a burden on society. Many countries in the developing world have large numbers of homeless children, as a result of widespread poverty, urban migration, and breakdowns in the social service sector following structural adjustments. In large Indian cities such as Mumbai, Kolkata, and New Delhi it is estimated that there are over 100,000 street children, many of whom are involved in drug use. In recent years, similar patterns have developed in Southeast Asia and Cambodia. Laos and Vietnam now have "substantial populations of street children [involved in] consuming drugs, living precariously with little or no family support or guardians". These homeless children receive no education or training that would allow them to participate in national development.

Anabolic Steroids

Anabolic steroids officially known as anabolic-androgenic steroids (AAS), are drugs which mimic the effects of the male steroids testosterone and dihydrotestosterone. They increase protein synthesis within cells, which results in the buildup of cellular tissue (anabolism), especially in muscles. Anabolic steroids also have androgenic and virilizing properties, including the development and maintenance of masculine characteristics such as the growth of the vocal cords and body hair. The word anabolic comes from the Greek anabolein, "to build up", and the word androgenic from the Greek andros, "man" + genein, "to produce".

Anabolic steroids were first isolated, identified and synthesized in the 1930s, and are now used therapeutically in medicine to stimulate bone growth and appetite, induce male puberty, and treat chronic wasting conditions, such as cancer and AIDS. The American College of Sports Medicine acknowledges that AAS, in the presence of adequate diet, can contribute to increases in body weight, often as lean mass increases, and that the gains in muscular strength achieved through high-intensity exercise and proper diet can be additionally increased by the use of AAS in some individuals.

Some health risks can be produced by long-term use or excessive doses of anabolic steroids. These effects include harmful changes in cholesterol levels, acne, high blood pressure, liver damage, and dangerous changes in the structure of the left ventricle of the heart.

The uses for anabolic steroids in sports and bodybuilding highly controversial, because of their adverse effects and the potential to gain an advantage conventionally considered "cheating." Their use is referred to as doping and banned by all major sporting bodies. For many years the AAS have been by far the most detected doping substances in IOC-accredited laboratories. In countries where AAS are controlled substances, there is often a black market in which smuggled or even counterfeit drugs are sold to users.

There are three common forms in which anabolic steroids are administered: oral pills, injectable steroids, and skin patches. Oral administration is the most convenient. Testosterone administered by mouth is rapidly absorbed, but it is largely converted to inactive metabolites, and only about 1/6 is available in active form. In order to be sufficiently active when given by mouth, testosterone derivatives are alkylated. This modification reduces the liver's ability to break down these compounds before they reach the systemic circulation.

Testosterone can be administered parenterally, but it has more prolonged absorption time and greater activity in propionate, enanthate, undecanoate or cypionate ester form. These derivatives are hydrolyzed to release free testosterone at the site of injection. Injectable steroids are typically administered into the muscle, not into the vein, to avoid sudden changes in the amount of the drug in the bloodstream.

Trans-dermal patches may also be used to deliver a steady dose through the skin and into the bloodstream. Injection is the most common method used by individuals administering anabolic steroids for non-medical purposes.

The traditional routes of administration do not have differential effects on the efficacy of the drug. Studies indicate that the anabolic properties of anabolic steroids are relatively similar despite the differences in pharmacokinetic principles such as first-pass metabolism. However, the orally available forms of AAS may cause liver damage in high doses.

The pharmacodynamics of anabolic steroids are unlike peptide hormones. Water-soluble peptide hormones cannot penetrate the fatty cell membrane and only indirectly affect the nucleus of target cells through their interaction with the cell's surface receptors. Conversely, as fat-soluble hormones, anabolic steroids are membrane permeable and influence the nucleus of cells by direct action.

The pharmacodynamic action of anabolic steroids begin when the exogenous hormone penetrates the membrane of the target cell and binds to an androgen receptor located in the cytoplasm of that cell. From there, the compound hormone-receptor diffuses into the nucleus, where it either alters the expression of genes or activates processes that send signals to other parts of the cell.

Different types of anabolic steroids bind to the androgen receptor with different affinities, depending on their chemical structure. Some anabolic steroids such as methandrostenolone bind weakly to this receptor in-vitro, but still exhibit androgenic effects in-vivo. The reason for this discrepancy is not known. On the other hand, steroids such as oxandrolone bind tightly to the receptor and act mostly on gene expression.

The effect of anabolic steroids on muscle mass is caused in at least two ways: first, they increase the production of proteins; second, they reduce recovery time by blocking the effects of stress hormone cortisol on muscle tissue, so that metabolism of muscle is greatly reduced. It has been hypothesized that this reduction in muscle breakdown may occur through anabolic steroids inhibiting the action of other steroid hormones called glucocorticoids that promote the breakdown of muscles.

Anabolic steroids also affect the number of cells that develop into fat-storage cells, by favoring cellular differentiation into muscle cells instead. Anabolic steroids can also decrease fat by increasing basal metabolic rate (BMR), since an increase in muscle mass increases BMR.

As the name suggests, anabolic-androgenic steroids have two different, but overlapping, types of effects: anabolic, meaning that they promote anabolism or cell growth, and androgenic or virilizing, meaning that they affect the development and maintenance of masculine characteristics.

Some examples of the anabolic effects of these hormones are increased protein synthesis from amino acids, increased appetite, increased bone remodeling and growth, and stimulation of bone marrow, which increases the production of red blood cells. Through a number of mechanisms anabolic steroids stimulate the formation of muscles cells and hence cause an increase in the size of skeletal muscles leading to increased strength.

The androgenic effects of AAS are numerous. Processes affected include pubertal growth, sebaceous gland oil production, and sexuality (especially in fetal development). Some examples of virilizing effects are growth of the clitoris in females and the penis in male children (the adult penis does not grow even when exposed to high doses of androgens), increased growth of androgen-sensitive hair (pubic, beard, chest, and limb hair), increased vocal cord size, deepening the voice, increased libido, suppression of natural sex hormones, and impaired production of sperm.

The androgenic:anabolic ratio of an AAS is an important factor when determining the clinical application of these compounds. Compounds with a high ratio of androgenic to a anabolic effects are the drug of choice in androgen-replacement therapy, whereas compounds with a reduced androgenic:anabolic ratio are preferred for anemia, osteoporosis, and to reverse protein loss following trauma, surgery or prolonged immobilization.

Determination of androgenic:anabolic ratio is typically performed in animal studies, which has led to the marketing of some compounds claimed to have anabolic activity with weak androgenic effects. This disassociation is less marked in humans, where all anabolic steroids have significant androgenic effects.

A commonly used protocol for determining the androgenic:anabolic ratio, dating back to the 1950s, uses the relative weights of ventral prostate (VP) and levator ani muscle (LA) of male rats. The VP weight is an indicator of the androgenic effect, while the LA weight is an indicator of the anabolic effect. Two or more batches of rats are castrated and given no treatment and respectively some AAS of interest. The LA/VP ratio for an AAS is calculated as the ratio of LA/VP weight gains produced by the treatment with that compound using castrated but untreated rats as baseline: (LAc,t-LAc)/(VPc,t-VPc). The LA/VP weight gain ratio from rat experiments is not unitary for testosterone, but it's normalized for presentation purposes, and used as basis of comparison for other AAS, which have their androgenic:anabolic ratios scaled accordingly. In the early 2000s this procedure was standardized and generalized throughout OECD in what is now known as the Hershberger assay.

A review spanning more than three decades of experimental studies in men found that body weight may increase by 2-5 kg as a result of short term (<10 weeks) AAS use, which may be attributed mainly to an increase of lean mass. Animal studies also found that fat mass was reduced, but most studies in humans failed to elucidate significant fat mass decrements. The effects on lean body mass have been shown to be dose dependent. Both muscle hypertrophy and the formation of new muscle fibers have been observed. The hydration of lean mass remains unaffected by AAS use, although small increments of blood volume cannot be ruled out.

The upper region of the body (thorax, neck, shoulders and upper arm) seems to be more susceptible for AAS than other body regions because of predominance of androgen receptors in the upper body. The largest difference in muscle fiber size between AAS users and non-users was observed in type I muscle fibers of the vastus lateralis and the trapezius muscle as a result of long-term AAS self-administration. After drug withdrawal the effects fade away slowly, but may persist for more than 6-12 weeks after cessation of AAS use.

The same review observed strength improvements in the range of 5-20% of baseline strength, largely depending on the drugs and dose used as well as the administration period. Overall, the exercise where the most significant improvements were observed was the bench press. For almost two decades it was assumed that AAS only exerted significant effects in experienced strength athletes.

In 1996 a randomized controlled trial published in the New England Journal of Medicine demonstrated however that even in novice athletes a 10-week strength training program accompanied by testosterone enanthate at 600 mg/week may improve strength more than training alone does. The same study found that dose was sufficient to significantly improve lean muscle mass relative to placebo even in subjects that did not exercise at all. A 2001 study by the same first author, showed that the anabolic effects of testosterone enanthate were highly dose dependent.

Anabolic steroids can cause many adverse effects. Most of these side effects are dose-dependent, the most common being elevated blood pressure, especially in those with pre-existing hypertension, and harmful changes in cholesterol levels: some steroids cause an increase in LDL cholesterol and a decrease in HDL cholesterol. Anabolic steroids have been shown to alter fasting blood sugar and glucose tolerance tests.

Anabolic steroids such as testosterone also increase the risk of cardiovascular disease or coronary artery disease. Acne is fairly common among anabolic steroid users, mostly due to stimulation of the sebaceous glands by increased testosterone levels. Conversion of testosterone to dihydrotestosterone (DHT) can accelerate the rate of premature baldness for males who are genetically predisposed, but testosterone itself can produce baldness in females.

High doses of oral anabolic steroid compounds can cause liver damage, as the steroids are metabolized in the digestive system to increase their bioavailability and stability.

There are also sex-specific side effects of anabolic steroids. Development of breast tissue in males, a condition called gynecomastia (which is usually caused by high levels of circulating estrogen), may arise because of increased conversion of testosterone to estrogen by the enzyme aromatase. Reduced sexual function and temporary infertility can also occur in males.

Another male-specific side effect which can occur is testicular atrophy, caused by the suppression of natural testosterone levels, which inhibits production of sperm (most of the mass of the testes is developing sperm). This side effect is temporary: the size of the testicles usually returns to normal within a few weeks of discontinuing anabolic steroid use as normal production of sperm resumes.

Female-specific side effects include increases in body hair, deepening of the voice, enlarged clitoris, and temporary decreases in menstrual cycles. When taken during pregnancy, anabolic steroids can affect fetal development by causing the development of male features in the female fetus and female features in the male fetus.

A number of severe side effects can occur if adolescents use anabolic steroids. For example, the steroids may prematurely stop the lengthening of bones, resulting in stunted growth. Other effects include, but are not limited to, accelerated bone maturation, increased frequency and duration of erections, and premature sexual development. Anabolic steroid use in adolescence is also correlated with poorer attitudes related to health.

Other side effects can include alterations in the structure of the heart, such as enlargement and thickening of the left ventricle, which impairs its contraction and relaxation. Possible effects of these alterations in the heart are hypertension, cardiac arrhythmia's, congestive heart failure, heart attacks, and sudden cardiac death. These changes are also seen in non-drug using athletes, but steroid use may accelerate this process. However, both the connection between changes in the structure of the left ventricle and decreased cardiac function, as well as the connection to steroid use have been disputed.

A 2005 review in CNS Drugs determined that "significant psychiatric symptoms including aggression and violence, mania, and less frequently psychosis and suicide have been associated with steroid abuse. Long-term steroid abusers may develop symptoms of dependence and withdrawal on discontinuation of AAS". High concentrations of AAS, comparable to those likely sustained by many recreational AAS users, produce apoptotic effects on neurons, raising the specter of possibly irreversible neuropsychiatric toxicity. Recreational AAS use appears to be associated with a range of potentially prolonged psychiatric effects, including dependence syndromes, mood disorders, and progression to other forms of substance abuse, but the prevalence and severity of these various effects remains poorly understood.

There is no evidence that steroid dependence develops from therapeutic use of anabolic steroids to treat medical disorders, but instances of AAS dependence have been reported among weightlifters and bodybuilders who chronically administered supraphysiologic doses. Mood disturbances are likely to be dose- and drug-dependent, but AAS dependence or withdrawal effects seem to occur only in a small number of AAS users.

Large scale long term studies of psychiatric effects on AAS users are generally not available. In 2003, the first naturalistic long term study on ten users, seven of which completed the study, found a high incidence of mood disorders and substance abuse, but few clinically relevant changes in physiological parameters or laboratory measures were noted throughout the study, and these changes were not clearly related to periods of reported AAS use. A 13-month study, published in 2006 and which involved 320 body builders and athletes suggests that the wide range of psychiatric side effects induced by the use of AAS is correlated to the severity of abuse.

From the mid-1980s onwards the popular press has been reporting "roid rage" as a side effect of AAS. A 2005 review determined that some, but not all, randomized controlled studies have found that anabolic steroid use correlates with hypomania and increased aggressiveness, but pointed out that attempts to determine whether AAS use triggers violent behavior have failed, primarily because of high rates of non-participation.

A 2008 study on a nationally representative sample of young adult males in the United States found an association between lifetime and past-year self-reported anabolic-androgenic steroid use and involvement in violent acts. Compared with individuals who did not use steroids, young adult males who used anabolic-androgenic steroids reported greater involvement in violent behaviors even after controlling for the effects of key demographic variables, previous violent behavior, and poly-drug use.

A 1996 review examining the blind studies available at that time also found that these had demonstrated a link between aggression and steroid use, but pointed out that with estimates of over one million past or current steroid users in the United States at that time, an extremely small percentage of those using steroids appear to have experienced mental disturbance severe enough to result in clinical treatments or medical case reports.

A 1996 randomized controlled trial, which involved 43 men, did not find an increase in the occurrence of angry behavior during 10 weeks of administration of testosterone enanthate at 600 mg/week, but this study screened out subjects that had previously abused steroids or had any psychiatric antecedents. A trial conducted in 2000 using testosterone cypionate at 600 mg/week found that treatment significantly increased manic scores on the YMRS, and aggressive responses on several scales. The drug response was highly variable, however: 84% of subjects exhibited minimal psychiatric effects, 12% became mildly hypomanic, and 4% became markedly hypomanic. The mechanism of these variable reactions could not be explained by demographic, psychological, laboratory, or physiological measures.

A 2006 study of two pairs of identical twins, in which one twin used anabolic steroids and the other did not, found that in both cases the steroid-using twin exhibited high levels of aggressiveness, hostility, anxiety and paranoid ideation not found in the "control" twin. A small scale study of 10 AAS users found that cluster B personality disorders were confounding factors for aggression. Yet this has not been proven by the medical community.

The legal status of anabolic steroids varies from country to country: some have stricter controls on their use or prescription than others though in many countries they are not illegal. In the U.S., anabolic steroids are currently listed as Schedule III controlled substances under the Controlled Substances Act, which makes the first offense simple possession of such substances without a prescription a federal crime punishable by up to one year in prison, and the unlawful distribution or possession with intent to distribute anabolic steroids punishable as a first offense by up to five years in prison (to be increased to ten years, effective on or about April 13, 2009).

In Canada, anabolic steroids and their derivatives are part of the Controlled drugs and substances act and are Schedule IV substances, meaning that it is illegal to obtain or sell them without a prescription; however, possession is not punishable, a consequence reserved for schedule I, II or III substances. Those guilty of buying or selling anabolic steroids in Canada can be imprisoned for up to 18 months. Import and export also carry similar penalties.

Anabolic steroids are also illegal without prescription in Australia, Argentina, Brazil and Portugal, and are listed as Class C Controlled Drugs in the United Kingdom. On the other hand, anabolic steroids are readily available without a prescription in some countries such as Mexico and Thailand.

The history of the U.S. legislation on anabolic steroids goes back to the late 1980s, when the U.S. Congress considered placing anabolic steroids under the Controlled Substances Act following the controversy over Ben Johnson's victory at the 1988 Summer Olympics in Seoul. During deliberations, the American Medical Association (AMA), Drug Enforcement Administration (DEA), Food and Drug Administration (FDA) as well as the National Institute on Drug Abuse (NIDA) all opposed listing anabolic steroids as controlled substances, citing the fact that use of these hormones does not lead to the physical or psychological dependence required for such scheduling under the Controlled Substance Act. Nevertheless, anabolic steroids were added to Schedule III of the Controlled Substances Act in the Anabolic Steroid Control Act of 1990.

The same act also introduced more stringent controls with higher criminal penalties for offenses involving the illegal distribution of anabolic steroids and human growth hormone. By the early 1990s, after anabolic steroids were scheduled in the U.S., several pharmaceutical companies stopped manufacturing or marketing the products in the U.S., including Ciba, Searle, Syntex and others. In the Controlled Substances Act, anabolic steroids are defined to be any drug or hormonal substance chemically and pharmacologically related to testosterone (other than estrogen, progestins, and corticosteroids) that promote muscle growth. The act was amended by the Anabolic Steroid Control Act of 2004, which added prohormones to the list of controlled substances, with effect from January 20, 2005.

Cannabis

Cannabis, also known as marijuana, among many other names, refers to any number of preparations of the Cannabis plant intended for use as a psychoactive drug. The most common form of cannabis used as a drug is the dried herbal form.

The typical herbal form of cannabis consists of the flowers and subtending leaves and stalks of mature pistillate or female plants. The resinous form of the drug is known as hashish (or merely as 'hash').

The major psychoactive chemical compound in cannabis is tetrahydrocannabinol (commonly abbreviated as THC). At least 66 other cannabinoids are also present in cannabis, including cannabidiol (CBD), cannabinol (CBN) and tetrahydrocannabivarin (THCV) among many others, which are believed to result in different effects than those of THC alone.

Cannabis use has been found to have occurred as long ago as the third millennium B.C. In modern times, the drug has been used for recreational, religious or spiritual, and medicinal purposes. The United Nations (UN) estimated that in 2004 about 4% of the world's adult population (162 million people) use cannabis annually, and about 0.6% (22.5 million) use it on a daily basis.

The possession, use, or sale of cannabis preparations containing psychoactive cannabinoids became illegal in most parts of the world in the early twentieth century. Since then, some countries have intensified the enforcement of cannabis prohibition, while others have reduced it.

Cannabis is indigenous to Central and South Asia. Evidence of the inhalation of cannabis smoke can be found as far back as the 3rd millennium B.C., as indicated by charred cannabis seeds found in a ritual brazier at an ancient burial site in present day Romania. Cannabis is also known to have been used by the ancient Hindus of India and Nepal thousands of years ago. The herb was called ganjika in Sanskrit (ganja in modern Indic languages). The ancient drug soma, mentioned in the Vedas as a sacred intoxicating hallucinogen, was sometimes associated with cannabis.

Cannabis was also known to the ancient Assyrians, who discovered its psychoactive properties through the Aryans. Using it in some religious ceremonies, they called it qunubu (meaning "way to produce smoke"), a probable origin of the modern word "cannabis". Cannabis was also introduced by the Aryans to the Scythians and Thracians/Dacians, whose shamans (the kapnobatai-"those who walk on smoke/clouds") burned cannabis flowers to induce a state of trance. Members of the cult of Dionysus, believed to have originated in Thrace (Bulgaria, Greece and Turkey), are also thought to have inhaled cannabis smoke. In 2003, a leather basket filled with cannabis leaf fragments and seeds was found next to a 2,500- to 2,800-year-old mummified shaman in the northwestern Xinjiang Uygur Autonomous Region of China.

Cannabis has an ancient history of ritual use and is found in pharmacological cults around the world. Hemp seeds discovered by archaeologists at Pazyryk suggest early ceremonial practices like eating by the Scythians occurred during the 5th to 2nd century B.C., confirming previous historical reports by Herodotus. One writer has claimed that cannabis was used as a religious sacrament by ancient Jews and early Christians due to the similarity between the Hebrew word "qannabbos" ("cannabis") and the Hebrew phrase "qené bósem" ("aromatic cane"). It was used by Muslims in various Sufi orders as early as the Mamluk period, for example by the Qalandars.

A study published in the South African Journal of Science showed that "pipes dug up from the garden of Shakespeare's home in Stratford Upon Avon contain traces of cannabis."The chemical analysis was carried out after researchers hypothesized that the 'noted weed' mentioned in Sonnet 76 and the 'journey in my head' from Sonnet 27 could be references to cannabis and the use thereof".

Cannabis was criminalized in the United States in 1937 due to Marihuana Tax Act of 1937. Several theories try to explain why it is illegal in most Western societies. Jack Herer, a cannabis legalization activist and writer, argues that the economic interests of the paper and chemical industry were a driving force to make it illegal. Another explanation is that beneficial effects of hemp would lower the profit of pharmaceutical companies which therefore have a vital interest to keep cannabis illegal.

Those economic theories were criticized for not taking social aspect into account. The outlawing was rather a result of racism directed to associate American immigrants of Mexican and African descent with cannabis abuse.

The terms cannabis or marijuana generally refer to the dried flowers and subtending leaves and stems of the female cannabis plant. This is the most widely consumed form, containing 3% to 22% THC. In contrast, cannabis strains used to produce industrial hemp contain less than 1% THC and are thus not valued for recreational use.

Hashish or hash is a concentrated resin produced from the flowers of the female cannabis plant. Hash can often be more potent than marijuana and can be smoked or chewed. It varies in color from black to golden brown depending upon purity.

According to both the "Talk to FRANK" website and the UKCIA website, "Soap Bar", "perhaps the most common type of hash found in the UK", can contain turpentine, tranquillizers, boot polish, henna and animal turds - amongst several other things. One small study of five soap-bar samples seized by UK Customs in 2001 found huge adulteration by many toxic substances, including soil, glue, engine oil and animal feces.

Because of THC's adhesive properties, a sticky residue builds up inside the paraphernalia when cannabis is smoked. It has tar-like properties but still contains THC as well as other cannabinoids. This buildup still has all the psychoactive properties of cannabis but is more difficult to smoke due to the discomfort caused to the throat and lungs. Cannabis users typically only smoke residue when cannabis is unavailable. Glass may be water-steamed at a low temperature prior to scraping in order to make the residue easier to remove.

According to the United Nations Office on Drugs and Crime (UNODC), "the amount of THC present in a cannabis sample is generally used as a measure of cannabis potency." The three main forms of cannabis products are the herb (marijuana), resin (hashish), and oil (hash oil). The UNODC states that marijuana often contains 5% THC content, resin "can contain up to 20% THC content", and that "Cannabis oil may contain more than 60% THC content.".

A scientific study published in 2000 in the Journal of Forensic Sciences (JFS) found that the potency (THC content) of confiscated cannabis in the United States (US) rose from "approximately 3.3% in 1983 and 1984", to "4.47% in 1997". It also concluded that "other major cannabinoids (i.e., CBD, CBN, and CBC)" (other chemicals in cannabis) "showed no significant change in their concentration over the years". More recent research undertaken at the University of Mississippi's Potency Monitoring Project has found that average THC levels in cannabis samples between 1975 and 2007 have increased from 4% in 1983 to 9.6% in 2007.

Australia's National Cannabis Prevention and Information Centre (NCPIC) states that the buds (flowers) of the female cannabis plant contain the highest concentration of THC, followed by the leaves. The stalks and seeds have "much lower THC levels". The UN states that the leaves can contain ten times less THC than the buds, and the stalks one hundred times less THC.

According to the "Talk to FRANK" (UK) website:

"Recently, there has been an increased availability of strong herbal cannabis, containing on average 2-3 times the amount of the active compound, tetrahydrocannabinol or THC, as compared to the traditional imported 'weed'. This strong cannabis includes: 'sinsemilla' (a bud grown in the absence of male plants and which has no seeds); 'homegrown'; 'skunk', which has a characteristic strong smell; and imported 'netherweed'...

...it may not be possible to tell whether a particular sample of 'skunk' or 'homegrown' or 'sinsemilla' will have a higher potency than an equal amount of traditional herbal cannabis.

Of course, "homegrown", "netherweed" and "sinsemilla" are not always "strong". The selection of "skunk" strains generally are, although not every strain of cannabis with a "characteristic strong smell" can be accurately named "skunk".

"Traditional herbal cannabis" or "weed", has on the whole, always been subjectively "strong" and thus FRANK leaves his website uncited.

Cannabis is consumed in many different ways, most of which involve inhaling smoke.

The most commonly used include screened bowls, bubblers (small pipes with water chambers), bongs, one-hitters, chillums, paper-wrapped joints and tobacco-leaf-wrapped blunts. Local methods differ by the preparation of the cannabis plant before use, the parts of the cannabis plant which are used, and the treatment of the smoke before inhalation.

A vaporizer heats herbal cannabis, which causes the active ingredients to evaporate into a gas without burning the plant material A lower proportion of toxic chemicals are released than by smoking, although this may vary depending on the design of the vaporizer and the temperature at which it is set. This method of consuming cannabis produces markedly different effects than smoking due to the flash points of different cannabinoids.

As an alternative to smoking, cannabis may be consumed orally. However, the cannabis or its extract must be sufficiently heated or dehydrated to cause decarboxylation of its most abundant cannabinoid, tetrahydrocannabinolic acid (THCA), into psychoactive THC.

Cannabinoids can be leached from cannabis plant matter using high-proof spirits (often grain alcohol) to create a tincture, often referred to as Green Dragon.

Cannabis can also be consumed as a tea. THC is lipophilic and only slightly water soluble so tea is made by first adding a saturated fat to hot water with a small amount of cannabis, green or black tea leaves and honey or sugar, steeped for approximately 5 minutes.

Cannabis has psychoactive and physiological effects when consumed. The minimum amount of THC required to have a perceptible psychoactive effect is about 10 micrograms per kilogram of body weight. Aside from a subjective change in perception and, most notably, mood, the most common short-term physical and neurological effects include increased heart rate, lowered blood pressure, impairment of short-term episodic memory, working memory, psycho-motor coordination, and concentration. Long-term effects are less clear.

A 2005 comprehensive review of the literature on the cannabis gateway hypothesis found that preexisting traits may predispose users to addiction in general, the availability of multiple drugs in a given setting confounds predictive patterns in their usage, and drug sub-cultures are more influential than cannabis itself. The study called for further research on "social context, individual characteristics, and drug effects" to discover the actual relationships between cannabis and the use of other drugs.

A new user of cannabis who feels there is a difference between anti-drug information and their own experiences will apply this distrust to public information about other, more powerful drugs. Some studies state that while there is no proof for this gateway hypothesis, young cannabis users should still be considered as a risk group for intervention programs. Other findings indicate that hard drug users are likely to be "poly-drug" users, and that interventions must address the use of multiple drugs instead of a single hard drug.

Another gateway hypothesis is that while cannabis is not as harmful or addictive as other drugs, a gateway effect may be detected as a result of the "common factors" involved with using any illegal drug. Because of its illegal status, cannabis users are more likely to be in situations which allow them to become acquainted with people who use and sell other illegal drugs.

By this argument, some studies have shown that alcohol and tobacco may be regarded as gateway drugs. However, a more parsimonious explanation could be that cannabis is simply more readily available (and at an earlier age) than illegal hard drugs, and alcohol/tobacco are in turn easier to obtain earlier than cannabis, though the reverse may be true in some areas, thus leading to the "gateway sequence" in those people who are most likely to experiment with any drug offered.

Since the beginning of the 20th century, most countries have enacted laws against the cultivation, possession, or transfer of cannabis for recreational use. These laws have impacted adversely on the cannabis plant's cultivation for non-recreational purposes, but there are many regions where, under certain circumstances, handling of cannabis is legal or licensed. Many jurisdictions have lessened the penalties for possession of small quantities of cannabis, so that it is punished by confiscation and sometimes a fine, rather than imprisonment, focusing more on those who traffic the drug on the black market.

In some areas where cannabis use has been historically tolerated, some new restrictions have been put in place, such as the closing of cannabis coffee shops near the borders of the Netherlands, closing of coffee shops near secondary schools in the Netherlands and crackdowns on "Pusher Street" in Christiania, Copenhagen in 2004.

Some jurisdictions use free voluntary treatment programs and/or mandatory treatment programs for frequent known users. Simple possession can carry long prison terms in some countries, particularly in East Asia, where the sale of cannabis may lead to a sentence of life in prison or even execution.

Opium

Opium is the dried latex obtained from opium poppies (Papaver somniferum). Opium contains up to 12% morphine, an opiate alkaloid, which is most frequently processed chemically to produce heroin for the illegal drug trade. The latex also includes codeine and non-narcotic alkaloids, such as papaverine, thebaine and noscapine. The latex is obtained by lacerating (or "scoring") the immature seed pods (fruits); the latex leaks out and dries to a sticky brown residue. This is scraped off the fruit. Meconium historically referred to related, weaker preparations made from other parts of the poppy or different species of poppies. Modern opium production is the culmination of millennia of production, in which the morphine content of the plants, methods of extraction and processing, and methods of consumption have become increasingly potent.

Cultivation of opium poppies for food, anesthesia, and ritual purposes dates back to at least the Neolithic Age. The Sumerian, Assyrian, Egyptian, Minoan, Greek, Roman, Persian and Arab Empires each made widespread use of opium, which was the most potent form of pain relief then available, allowing ancient surgeons to perform prolonged surgical procedures. Opium is mentioned in the most important medical texts of the ancient world, including the Ebers Papyrus and the writings of Dioscorides, Galen, and Avicenna.

Widespread medical use of unprocessed opium continued through the American Civil War before giving way to morphine and its successors, which could be injected at a precisely controlled dosage. American morphine is still produced primarily from poppies grown and processed in India in the traditional manner and remains the standard of pain relief for casualties of war.

In China recreational use of the drug began in the fifteenth century but was limited by its rarity and expense. Opium trade became more regular by the seventeenth century, when it was mixed with tobacco for smoking, and addiction was first recognized. Opium prohibition in China began in 1729 yet was followed by nearly two centuries of increasing opium use. China had a positive balance sheet in trading with the British, which led to a decrease of the British silver stocks. Therefore, the British tried to encourage Chinese opium use to enhance their balance, and they delivered it from Indian provinces under British control.

A massive confiscation of opium by the Chinese emperor, who tried to stop the opium deliveries, led to two Opium Wars in 1839 and 1858, in which Britain suppressed China and traded opium all over the country. After 1860, opium use continued to increase with widespread domestic production in China, until more than a quarter of the male population was addicted by 1905. Recreational or addictive opium use in other nations remained rare into the late nineteenth century, recorded by an ambivalent literature that sometimes praised the drug.

Global regulation of opium began with the stigmatization of Chinese immigrants and opium dens in San Francisco, California, leading rapidly from town ordinances in the 1870s to the formation of the International Opium Commission in 1909. During this period, the portrayal of opium in literature became squalid and violent, British opium trade was largely supplanted by domestic Chinese production, purified morphine and heroin became widely available for injection, and patent medicines containing opiates reached a peak of popularity. Opium was prohibited in many countries during the early twentieth century, leading to the modern pattern of opium production as a precursor for illegal recreational drugs or tightly regulated legal prescription drugs.

Illicit opium production, now dominated by Afghanistan, was decimated in 2000 when production was banned by the Taliban, but has increased steadily since the fall of the Taliban in 2001 and over the course of the War in Afghanistan. Worldwide production in 2006 was 6610 metric tons - nearly one-fifth the level of production in 1906. Opium for illegal use is often converted into heroin, which multiplies its potency to approximately twice that of morphine, can be taken by intravenous injection, and is easier to smuggle.

At least seventeen finds of Papaver somniferum from Neolithic settlements have been reported throughout Switzerland, Germany, and Spain, including the placement of large numbers of poppy seed capsules at a burial site (the Cueva de los Murciélagos, or "Bat cave," in Spain), which have been carbon-14 dated to 4200 B.C.

Numerous finds of Papaver somniferum or Papaver setigerum from Bronze Age and Iron Age settlements have also been reported. The first known cultivation of opium poppies was in Mesopotamia, approximately 3400 B.C., by Sumerians who called the plant Hul Gil, the "joy plant". Tablets found at Nippur, a Sumerian spiritual center south of Baghdad, described the collection of poppy juice in the morning and its use in production of opium.

Cultivation continued in the Middle East by the Assyrians, who also collected poppy juice in the morning after scoring the pods with an iron scoop; they called the juice aratpa-pal, possibly the root of Papaver. Opium production continued under the Babylonians and Egyptians.

Opium was used with poison hemlock to put people quickly and painlessly to death, but it was also used in medicine. The Ebers Papyrus, ca. 1500 B.C., describes a way to "stop a crying child" using grains of the poppy-plant strained to a pulp. Spongia somnifera, sponges soaked in opium, were used during surgery. The Egyptians cultivated opium thebaicum in famous poppy fields around 1300 B.C.

Opium was traded from Egypt by the Phoenicians and Minoans to destinations around the Mediterranean Sea, including Greece, Carthage, and Europe. By 1100 B.C., opium was cultivated on the Mediterranean island of Cyprus, where surgical-quality knives were used to score the poppy pods, and opium was cultivated, traded, and smoked. Opium was also mentioned after the Persian conquest of Assyria and Babylonia in the sixth century B.C.

From the earliest finds, opium has appeared to have ritual significance, and anthropologists have speculated that ancient priests may have used the drug as a proof of healing power. In Egypt, the use of opium was generally restricted to priests, magicians, and warriors, its invention credited to Thoth, and it was said to have been given by Isis to Ra as treatment for a headache.

A figure of the Minoan "goddess of the narcotics," wearing a crown of three opium poppies, ca. 1300 B.C., was recovered from the Sanctuary of Gazi, Crete, together with a simple smoking apparatus. The Greek gods Hypnos (Sleep), Nyx (Night), and Thanatos (Death) were depicted wreathed in poppies or holding poppies. Poppies also frequently adorned statues of Apollo, Asklepios, Pluto, Demeter, Aphrodite, Kybele and Isis, symbolizing nocturnal oblivion.

As the power of the Roman Empire declined, the lands to the south, and east of the Mediterranean sea became incorporated into the Islamic Empire, which assembled the finest libraries and the most skilled physicians of the era. Many Muslims believe that the hadith of al-Bukhari prohibits every intoxicating substance as haraam, but the use of intoxicants in medicine has been widely permitted by Scholars, even though it is prohibited under Islamic Law. Dioscorides' five-volume De Materia Medica, the precursor of pharmacopoeias, remained in use (with some improvements in Arabic versions) from the 1st to 16th centuries and described opium, meconium and the wide range of uses prevalent in the ancient world.

Somewhere between 400 and 1200 AD, Arab traders introduced opium to China. The Persian physician Abu Bakr Muhammad ibn Zakariya al-Razi Rhazes (845-930 A.D.) maintained a laboratory and school in Baghdad, and was a student and critic of Galen, made use of opium in anesthesia and recommended its use for the treatment of melancholy in Fi ma-yahdara al-tabib (In the Absence of a Physician) , a home medical manual directed toward ordinary citizens for self-treatment if a doctor was not available.

The renowned ophthalmologic surgeon Abu al-Qasim Ammar (936-1013 AD) relied on opium and mandrake as surgical anaesthetics and wrote a treatise, al-Tasrif, that influenced medical thought well into the sixteenth century. The Persian physician Abū 'Alī al-Husayn ibn Sina (Avicenna) described opium as the most powerful of the stupefacients, by comparison with mandrake and other highly effective herbs, in The Canon of Medicine. This classic text was translated into Latin in 1175 and later into many other languages and remained authoritative into the seventeenth century. Şerafeddin Sabuncuoğlu used opium in the fourteenth century Ottoman Empire to treat migraine headaches, sciatica, and other painful ailments.

Opium became stigmatized in Europe during the Inquisition as a Middle Eastern influence and became a taboo subject in Europe from approximately 1300 to 1500 A.D. Manuscripts of Pseudo-Apuleius's fifth-century work from the tenth and eleventh centuries refer to the use of wild poppy Papaver agreste or Papaver rhoeas (identified as Papaver silvaticum) instead of Papaver somniferum for inducing sleep and relieving pain.

The use of Paracelsus' laudanum was introduced to Western medicine in 1527, when Philip Aureolus Theophrastus Bombast von Hohenheim, better known by the name Paracelsus, returned from his wanderings in Arabia with a famous sword, within the pommel of which he kept "Stones of Immortality" compounded from opium thebaicum, citrus juice, and "quintessence of gold".

The name "Paracelsus" was a pseudonym signifying him the equal or better of Aulus Cornelius Celsus, whose text, which described the use of opium or a similar preparation, had recently been translated and reintroduced to medieval Europe. The Canon of Medicine, the standard medical textbook that Paracelsus burned in a public bonfire three weeks after being appointed professor at the University of Basel, also described the use of opium, though many Latin translations were of poor quality.

Laudanum was originally the sixteenth-century term for a medicine associated with a particular physician that was widely well-regarded, but became standardized as "tincture of opium," a solution of opium in ethyl alcohol, which Paracelsus has been credited with developing. During his lifetime, Paracelsus was viewed as an adventurer who challenged the theories and mercenary motives of contemporary medicine with dangerous chemical therapies, but his therapies marked a turning point in Western medicine. In the seventeenth century laudanum was recommended for pain, sleeplessness, and diarrhea by Thomas Sydenham, the renowned "father of English medicine" or "English Hippocrates," to whom is attributed the quote, "Among the remedies which it has pleased Almighty God to give to man to relieve his sufferings, none is so universal and so efficacious as opium". Use of opium as a cure-all was reflected in the formulation of mithridatium described in the 1728 Chambers Cyclopedia, which included true opium in the mixture. Subsequently, laudanum became the basis of many popular patent medicines of the nineteenth century.

The standard medical use of opium persisted well into the nineteenth century. U.S. president William Henry Harrison was treated with opium in 1841, and in the American Civil War, the Union Army used 2.8 million ounces of opium tincture and powder and about 500,000 opium pills. During this time of popularity, users called opium "God's Own Medicine".

The most important reason for the increase in opiate consumption in the United States during the 19th century was the prescribing and dispensing of legal opiates by physicians and pharmacist to women with "female problems", mostly to relieve painful menstruation. Between 150,000 and 200,000 opiate addicts lived in the United States in the late 19th century and between two-thirds and three-quarters of these addicts were women.

There were no legal restrictions on the importation or use of opium in the United States until the San Francisco, California, Opium Den Ordinance, which banned dens for public smoking of opium in 1875, a measure fueled by anti-Chinese sentiment and the perception that whites were starting to frequent the dens. This was followed by an 1891 California law requiring that narcotics carry warning labels and that their sales be recorded in a registry, amendments to the California Pharmacy and Poison Act in 1907 making it a crime to sell opiates without a prescription, and bans on possession of opium or opium pipes in 1909.

At the US federal level, the legal actions taken reflected constitutional restrictions under the Enumerated powers doctrine prior to reinterpretation of the Commerce clause, which did not allow the federal government to enact arbitrary prohibitions but did permit arbitrary taxation. Beginning in 1883, opium importation was taxed at $6 to $300 per pound, until the Opium Exclusion Act of 1909 prohibited the importation of opium altogether. In a similar manner the Harrison Narcotics Tax Act of 1914, passed in fulfillment of the International Opium Convention of 1912, nominally placed a tax on the distribution of opiates, but served as a de facto prohibition of the drugs. Today, opium is regulated by the Drug Enforcement Administration under the Controlled Substances Act.

Following passage of a regional law in 1895, Australia's Aboriginal Protection and restriction of the sale of opium act 1897 addressed opium addiction among Aborigines, though it soon became a general vehicle for depriving them of basic rights by administrative regulation. Opium sale was prohibited to the general population in 1905, and smoking and possession was prohibited in 1908.

Hardening of Canadian attitudes toward Chinese opium users and fear of a spread of the drug into the white population led to the effective criminalization of opium for non-medical use in Canada between 1908 and the mid-1920s.

In 1909, the International Opium Commission was founded, and by 1914, thirty-four nations had agreed that the production and importation of opium should be diminished. In 1924, sixty-two nations participated in a meeting of the Commission. Subsequently, this role passed to the League of Nations, and all signatory nations agreed to prohibit the import, sale, distribution, export, and use of all narcotic drugs, except for medical and scientific purposes. This role was later taken up by the International Narcotics Control Board of the United Nations under Article 23 of the Single Convention on Narcotic Drugs, and subsequently under the Convention on Psychotropic Substances. Opium-producing nations are required to designate a government agency to take physical possession of licit opium crops as soon as possible after harvest and conduct all wholesaling and exporting through that agency.

Opium has gradually been superseded by a variety of purified, semi-synthetic, and synthetic opioids with progressively stronger effect, and by other general anesthetics. This process began in 1804, when Friedrich Wilhelm Adam Sertürner first isolated morphine from the opium poppy. The process continued until 1817, when Sertürner published the isolation of pure morphine from opium after at least thirteen years of research and a nearly disastrous trial on himself and three boys. The great advantage of purified morphine was that a patient could be treated with a known dose-whereas with raw plant material, as Gabriel Fallopius once lamented, "if soporifics are weak they do not help; if they are strong they are exceedingly dangerous".

Morphine was the first pharmaceutical isolated from a natural product, and this success encouraged the isolation of other alkaloids: by 1820, the isolation of narcotine, strychnine, veratrine, colchicine, caffeine, and quinine were reported. Morphine sales began in 1827, by Heinrich Emanuel Merck of Darmstadt, and helped him expand his family pharmacy into the Merck KGaA pharmaceutical company.

The use of diethyl ether and chloroform for general anesthesia began in 1846-1847, and rapidly displaced the use of opiates and tropane alkaloids from Solanaceae due to their relative safety.

Heroin, the first semi-synthetic opiate, was first synthesized in 1874, but was not pursued until its rediscovery in 1897 by Felix Hoffmann at the Bayer pharmaceutical company in Elberfeld, Germany. From 1898 to 1910 heroin was marketed as a non-addictive morphine substitute and cough medicine for children. By 1902, sales made up 5% of the company's profits, and "heroinism" had attracted media attention. Oxycodone, a thebaine derivative similar to codeine, was introduced by Bayer in 1916 and promoted as a less-addictive analgesic. Preparations of the drug such as Percocet and OxyContin remain popular to this day.

A range of synthetic opioids such as methadone (1937), pethidine (1939), fentanyl (late 1950s), and derivatives thereof have been introduced, and each is preferred for certain specialized applications. Nonetheless, morphine remains the drug of choice for American combat medics, who carry packs of syrettes containing 16 milligrams each for use on severely wounded soldiers. No drug has yet been found that can match the painkilling effect of opioids without also duplicating much of its addictive potential.

Opium production has fallen greatly since 1906, when 41,000 tons were produced, but because 39,000 tons of that year's opium were consumed in China, overall usage in the rest of the world was much lower. In 1980, 2,000 tons of opium supplied all legal and illegal uses.

Recently, opium production has increased considerably, surpassing 5,000 tons in 2002. In 2002, the price for one kilogram of opium was $300 for the farmer, $800 for purchasers in Afghanistan, and $16,000 on the streets of Europe before conversion into heroin.

Following documented trends of increasing availability mirroring increased American military and geopolitical regional involvement, Afghanistan is currently the primary producer of the drug. After regularly producing 70% of the world's opium, Afghanistan decreased production to 74 tons per year under a ban by the Taliban in 2000, a move which cut production by 94 per cent. A year later, after American and British troops invaded Afghanistan, removed the Taliban and installed the interim government, the land under cultivation jumped back to 285 square miles, with Afghanistan supplanting Burma to become the world's largest opium producer once more. Opium production in that country has increased rapidly since, reaching an all-time high in 2006.

According to DEA statistics, Afghanistan's production of oven-dried opium increased to 1,278 tons in 2002, more than doubled by 2003, and nearly doubled again during 2004. In late 2004, the U.S. government estimated that 206,000 hectares were under poppy cultivation, 4.5% of the country's total cropland, and produced 4,200 metric tons of opium, 76% of the world's supply, yielding 60% of Afghanistan's gross domestic product.

In 2006, the UN Office on Drugs and Crime estimated production to have risen 59% to 407,000 acres (1,650 km2) in cultivation, yielding 6,100 tons of opium, 82% of the world's supply. The value of the resulting heroin was estimated at $3.5 billion, of which Afghan farmers were estimated to have received $700 million in revenue (of which the Taliban have been estimated to have collected anywhere from tens of millions to $140 million in taxes). For farmers, the crop can be up to ten times more profitable than wheat. The price of opium is around $138 per kilo. However, opium production has led to rising tensions in Afghan villages. Though direct conflict has yet to occur, the opinions of the new class of young, rich men involved in the opium trade are at odds with those of the traditional village leaders.

An increasingly large fraction of opium is processed into morphine base and heroin in drug labs in Afghanistan. Despite an international set of chemical controls designed to restrict availability of acetic anhydride, it enters the country, perhaps through its Central Asian neighbors which do not participate. A counter-narcotics law passed in December 2005 requires Afghanistan to develop registries or regulations for tracking, storing, and owning acetic anhydride.

Besides Afghanistan, smaller quantities of opium are produced in Pakistan, the Golden Triangle region of Southeast Asia (particularly Myanmar), Colombia and Mexico.

Chinese production mainly trades and profits off of North America. In 2002, they were seeking to expand through eastern United States. Due to post 9/11 era, trading between borders became difficult and because new international laws were set into place, opium trade became more diffused. Power shifted from remote to high-end smugglers and opuim traders. Outsourcing became a huge factor for survival for many smugglers and opium farmers.

There is a longstanding literary history by and about opium users. Thomas de Quincey's 1822 Confessions of an English Opium-Eater is one of the first and most famous literary accounts of opium addiction written from the point of view of an addict and details both the pleasures and the dangers of the drug. De Quincey writes about the great English Romantic poet Samuel Taylor Coleridge (1772-1834), whose poem "Kubla Khan" is also widely considered to be a poem of the opium experience.

Coleridge began using opium in 1791 after developing jaundice and rheumatic fever and became a full addict after a severe attack of the disease in 1801, requiring 80-100 drops of laudanum daily. George Crabbe is another early writer who wrote about opium. "The Lotos-Eaters," an 1832 poem by Alfred Lord Tennyson, reflects the generally favorable British attitude toward the drug. In The Count of Monte Cristo (1844) by Alexandre Dumas, père, the Count is assuaged by an edible form of opium, and his experience with it is depicted vividly.

Edgar Allan Poe presents opium in a more disturbing context in his 1838 short story "Ligeia," in which the narrator, deeply distraught for the loss of his beloved, takes solace in opium until he "had become a bounden slave in the trammels of opium," unable to distinguish fantasy from reality after taking immoderate doses of opium.

In music, Hector Berlioz' 1830 Symphony Fantastique tells the tale of an artist who has poisoned himself with opium while in the depths of despair for a hopeless love. Each of the symphony's five movements takes place at a different setting and with increasingly audible effects from the drug. For example, in the fourth movement, "Marche au Supplice," the artist dreams that he is walking to his own execution. In the fifth movement, "Songe d'une Nuit du Sabbat," he dreams that he is at a witch's orgy, where he witnesses his beloved dancing wildly along to the demented Dies Irae.

Towards the end of the nineteenth century, references to opium and opium addiction in the context of crime and the foreign underclass abound within English literature, such as in Wilkie Collins' The Moonstone (1868), where it is used to attempt to uncover the jewel thief.

Opium features in the opening paragraphs of Charles Dickens's 1870 serial The Mystery of Edwin Drood and in Arthur Conan Doyle's 1891 Sherlock Holmes short story "The Man with the Twisted Lip." In Oscar Wilde's 1890 The Picture of Dorian Gray, the protagonist visits an opium den "for forgetfulness," unable to bear the guilt and shame of committing murder.

Opium likewise underwent a transformation in Chinese literature, becoming associated with indolence and vice by the early twentieth century. Perhaps the best-known literary reference to opium is Karl Marx's metaphor in his "Contribution to the Critique of Hegel's 'Philosophy of Right'," where he refers to religion as "the opium of the people." This phrase is more commonly quoted as "the opiate of the masses".

In the twentieth century, as the use of opium was eclipsed by morphine and heroin, its role in literature became more limited, and often focused on issues related to its prohibition. In The Good Earth by Pearl S. Buck, Wang Lung, the protagonist, gets his troublesome uncle and aunt addicted to opium in order to keep them out of his hair.

William S. Burroughs autobiographically describes the use of opium beside that of its derivatives. His associate Jack Black's memoir You Can't Win chronicles one man's experience both as an onlooker in the opium dens of San Francisco, and later as a "hop fiend" himself. The book and subsequent movie The Wonderful Wizard of Oz may allude to opium at one point in the story, when Dorothy and her friends are drawn into a field of poppies, in which they fall asleep.

Heroin

Heroin, or diacetylmorphine (INN), also known as diamorphine (BAN), is a semi-synthetic opioid drug synthesized from morphine, a derivative of the opium poppy. It is the 3,6-diacetyl ester of morphine (di (two)-acetyl-morphine). The white crystalline form is commonly the hydrochloride salt diacetylmorphine hydrochloride, though often adulterated thus dulling the sheen and consistency from that to a matte white powder, which however heroin freebase typically is.

As with other opioids, heroin is used as both a pain-killer and a recreational drug and has an extremely high potential for abuse. Frequent and regular administration is associated with tolerance, moderate physical dependence, and severe psychological dependence.

Internationally, heroin is controlled under Schedules I and IV of the Single Convention on Narcotic Drugs. It is illegal to manufacture, possess, or sell diacetylmorphine without a license in Belgium, Denmark, Germany, Iran, India, the Netherlands, the United States, Australia, Canada, Ireland, Pakistan, the United Kingdom and Swaziland.

Under the name diamorphine, it is a legally prescribed controlled drug in the United Kingdom. It is available for prescription to long-term users in the Netherlands, the United Kingdom, Switzerland, Germany and Denmark alongside psycho-social care, and a similar program is being campaigned for by liberal political parties in Norway.

The German drug company Bayer named its new over the counter drug "Heroin" in 1895. The name was derived from the German word "heroisch", meaning heroic, due to its perceived "heroic" effects upon a user. However, it was chiefly developed as a morphine substitute for the coughs that did not have its addictive side-effects.

Morphine at the time was a popular, but addictive recreational drug, so Bayer wanted to find a similar, but non-addictive substitute to market. However, contrary to Bayer's advertising as a "non-addictive morphine substitute," heroin would soon have one of the highest rates of dependence amongst its users.

When taken orally, diacetylmorphine undergoes extensive first-pass metabolism via deacetylation, making it a pro-drug for the systemic delivery of morphine. When the drug is injected, however, it avoids this first-pass effect, very rapidly crossing the blood-brain barrier due to the presence of the acetyl groups, which render it much more lipid-soluble than morphine itself. Once in the brain, it then is deacetylated into 6-monoacetylmorphine (6-MAM) and morphine which bind to μ-opioid receptors, resulting in the drug's euphoric, analgesic (pain relief), and anxiolytic (anti-anxiety) effects; diacetylmorphine itself exhibits relatively low affinity for the μ receptor. Unlike hydromorphone and oxymorphone, however, administered intravenously, diacetylmorphine creates a larger histamine release, similar to morphine, resulting in the feeling of a greater subjective "body high" to some, but also instances of pruritus (itching) when they first start using.

Both morphine and 6-MAM are μ-opioid agonists which bind to receptors present throughout the brain, spinal cord and gut of all mammals. The μ-opioid receptor also binds endogenous opioid peptides such as β-endorphin, Leu-enkephalin, and Met-enkephalin. Repeated use of diacetylmorphine results in a number of physiological changes, including decreases in the number of μ-opioid receptors.

These physiological alterations lead to tolerance and dependence, so that cessation of diacetylmorphine use results in a set of extremely uncomfortable symptoms including pain, anxiety, muscle spasms, and insomnia called the opioid withdrawal syndrome. Depending on usage it has an onset 4 to 24 hours after the last dose of diacetylmorphine. Morphine also binds to δ- and κ-opioid receptors.

There is also evidence that 6-MAM binds to a subtype of μ-opioid receptors which are also activated by the morphine metabolite morphine-6β-glucuronide but not morphine itself. The contribution of these receptors to the overall pharmacology of heroin remains unknown.

A subclass of morphine derivatives, namely the 3,6 esters of morphine, with similar effects and uses includes the clinically-used strong analgesics nicomorphine (Vilan), and dipropanoylmorphine; there is also the latter's dihydromorphine analogue, diacetyldihydromorphine (Paralaudin).

Under the name diamorphine, heroin is prescribed as a strong analgesic in the United Kingdom, where it is given via subcutaneous, intramuscular, intrathecal or intravenous route. Its use includes treatment for acute pain, such as in severe physical trauma, myocardial infarction, post-surgical pain, and chronic pain, including end-stage cancer and other terminal illnesses. In other countries it is more common to use morphine or other strong opioids in these situations.

In 2005, there was a shortage of diamorphine in the UK, due to a problem at the main UK manufacturers. Due to this, many hospitals changed to using morphine instead of diamorphine. Although there is no longer a problem with the manufacturing of heroine in the UK, many hospitals there have continued to use morphine.

Diamorphine continues to be widely used in palliative care in the United Kingdom, where it is commonly given by the subcutaneous route, often via a syringe driver, if patients could not easily swallow oral morphine solution. The advantage of diamorphine over morphine is that diamorphine is more soluble and smaller volumes of diamorphine are needed for the same analgesic effect. Both of these factors are advantageous if giving high doses of opioids via the subcutaneous route, which is often necessary in palliative care.

The medical use of diamorphine (in common with other strong opioids such as morphine, fentanyl and oxycodone) is controlled in the United Kingdom by the Misuse of Drugs Act 1971. In the UK, it is a class A controlled drug. Registers of its use are required to be kept in hospitals.

Heroin is also used as a maintenance drug in the treatment of heroin addicts. Though this is somewhat controversial among proponents of a zero tolerance drug policy it has proven superior to methadone in improving the social and health situation of addicts.

Diacetylmorphine is used as a recreational drug for the transcendent relaxation and intense euphoria it induces. Anthropologist Michael Agar once described heroin as "the perfect whatever drug". Tolerance quickly develops, and users need more of the drug to achieve the same effects. Its popularity with recreational drug users, compared to morphine, reportedly stems from its perceived different effects. In particular, users report an intense rush that occurs while the diacetylmorphine is being metabolized into 6-monoacetylmorphine (6-MAM) and morphine in the brain. Diacetylmorphine produces more euphoria than other opioids upon njection. One possible explanation is the presence of 6-monoacetylmorphine, a metabolite unique to diacetylmorphine. While other opioids of recreational use, such as codeine, produce only morphine, heroin also leaves 6-MAM, also a psycho-active metabolite. However, this perception is not supported by the results of clinical studies comparing the physiological and subjective effects of injected diacetylmorphine and morphine in individuals formerly addicted to opioids; these subjects showed no preference for one drug over the other.

Equipotent, injected doses had comparable action courses, with no difference in subjects' self-rated feelings of euphoria, ambition, nervousness, relaxation, drowsiness, or sleepiness. Short-term addiction studies by the same researchers demonstrated that tolerance developed at a similar rate to both diacetylmorphine and morphine. When compared to the opioids hydromorphone, fentanyl, oxycodone, and pethidine/meperidine, former addicts showed a strong preference for diacetylmorphine and morphine, suggesting that diacetylmorphine and morphine are particularly susceptible to abuse and addiction. Morphine and diacetylmorphine were also much more likely to produce euphoria and other positive subjective effects when compared to these other opioids.

One of the most common methods of illicit heroin use is via intravenous injection, colloquially termed "slamming" or "shooting up". Heroin base, commonly found in the UK and Europe, when prepared for injection will only dissolve in water when mixed with an acid. Most commonly citric acid powder or lemon juice is used and heated. Heroin in the US is most commonly its hydrochloride salt, requiring just water to dissolve. Users tend to initially inject in the easily accessible veins in the arm, but as these veins collapse over time through damage caused by the acid, the user will often resort to injecting in other veins.

Recreational users may also administer the drug through snorting, or smoking by inhaling its vapors when heated; either with tobacco in a rolled cigarette or by heating the drug on aluminum foil from underneath. When heated the heroin powder changes to a thick liquid, similar in consistency to molten wax, and it will run across the foil giving off smoke which the user inhales through a tube, usually made from foil also so that any heroin that collects on the inside of the tube can be smoked afterward. This method of administration is known as chasing the dragon. This should not be confused with smoking methamphetamine, which is known as "chasing the white dragon".

The onset of diacetylmorphine's effects depends upon the route of administration. Studies have shown that the subjective pleasure of drug use (the reinforcing component of addiction) is proportional to the rate at which the blood level of the drug increases. Intravenous injection provides the fastest and most intense rush within 7 to 8 seconds. Intramuscular injection produces a relatively slow onset of 5 to 8 minutes. Snorting or smoking reaches peak effects within 10 to 15 minutes. If taken orally, the effects take approximately half an hour to set in, with an absence of a rush.

The diacetylmorphine dose used for recreational purposes is dependent on the frequency and level of use. A first-time user may ingest between 5 and 20 mg of diacetylmorphine, while an addict may require several hundred mg per day.

Large doses of heroin can cause fatal respiratory depression, and the drug has been used for suicide or as a murder weapon. The serial killer Dr Harold Shipman used it on his victims as did Dr John Bodkin Adams (see his victim, Edith Alice Morrell). Because significant tolerance to respiratory depression develops quickly with continued use and is lost just as quickly during withdrawal, it is often difficult to determine whether a heroin death was an accident, suicide or murder. Examples include the overdose deaths of Sid Vicious, Janis Joplin, Tim Buckley, Layne Staley, Bradley Nowell, Ted Binion, and River Phoenix.

The origins of the present international illegal heroin trade can be traced back to laws passed in many countries in the early 1900s that closely regulated the production and sale of opium and its derivatives including heroin. At first, heroin flowed from countries where it was still legal into countries where it was no longer legal.

By the mid-1920s, heroin production had been made illegal in many parts of the world. An illegal trade developed at that time between heroin labs in China (mostly in Shanghai and Tianjin) and other nations. The weakness of government in China and conditions of civil war enabled heroin production to take root there. Chinese triad gangs eventually came to play a major role in the heroin trade. The French Connection route started in the 1930s.

Heroin trafficking was virtually eliminated in the U.S. during World War II due to temporary trade disruptions caused by the war. Japan's war with China had cut the normal distribution routes for heroin and the war had generally disrupted the movement of opium.

After World War II, the Mafia took advantage of the weakness of the postwar Italian government and set up heroin labs in Sicily. The Mafia took advantage of Sicily's location along the historic route opium took westward into Europe and the United States.

Large scale international heroin production effectively ended in China with the victory of the communists in the civil war in the late 1940s. The elimination of Chinese production happened at the same time that Sicily's role in the trade developed.

Although it remained legal in some countries until after World War II, health risks, addiction, and widespread recreational use led most western countries to declare heroin a controlled substance by the latter half of the 20th century.

In late 1960s and early 70s, the CIA supported anti-Communist Chinese Nationalists settled near Sino-Burmese border and Hmong tribesmen in Laos. This helped the development of the Golden Triangle opium production region, which supplied about one-third of heroin consumed in US after 1973 American withdrawal from Vietnam. As of 1999, Myanmar (formerly Burma), the heartland of the Golden Triangle remained second largest producer of heroin, after Afghanistan.

Soviet-Afghan war led to increased production in the Pakistani-Afghani border regions, as U.S.-backed mujaheddin militants raised money for arms from selling opium, contributing heavily to the modern Golden Crescent creation. By 1980, 60% of heroin sold in the U.S. originated in Afghanistan. It increased international production of heroin at lower prices in the 1980s. The trade shifted away from Sicily in the late 1970s as various criminal organizations violently fought with each other over the trade. The fighting also led to a stepped up government law enforcement presence in Sicily.

Traffic is heavy worldwide, with the biggest producer being Afghanistan. According to U.N. sponsored survey, as of 2004, Afghanistan accounted for production of 87 percent of the world's heroin. Afghan opium kills 100,000 people every year worldwide.

The cultivation of opium in Afghanistan reached its peak in 1999, when 225,000 acres-350 square miles-of poppies were sown. The following year the Taliban banned poppy cultivation, a move which cut production by 94 percent. By 2001 only 30 square miles of land were in use for growing opium poppies. A year later, after American and British troops had removed the Taliban and installed the interim government, the land under cultivation jumped back to 285 square miles, with Afghanistan supplanting Burma to become the world's largest opium producer once more. Opium production in that country has increased rapidly since, reaching an all-time high in 2006. War in Afghanistan once again appeared as a facilitator of the trade. Some 3.3 million Afghans are involved in producing opium.

At present, opium poppies are mostly grown in Afghanistan, and in Southeast Asia, especially in the region known as the Golden Triangle straddling Myanmar, Thailand, Vietnam, Laos and Yunnan province in the People's Republic of China. There is also cultivation of opium poppies in the Sinaloa region of Mexico and in Colombia. The majority of the heroin consumed in the United States comes from Mexico and Colombia. Up until 2004, Pakistan was considered one of the biggest opium-growing countries.

Conviction for trafficking in heroin carries the death penalty in most Southeast Asian, some East Asian and Middle Eastern countries, among which Malaysia, Singapore and Thailand are the most strict. The penalty applies even to citizens of countries where the penalty is not in place, sometimes causing controversy when foreign visitors are arrested for trafficking, for example the arrest of nine Australians in Bali, the death sentence given to Nola Blake in Thailand in 1987, or the hanging of an Australian citizen Van Tuong Nguyen in Singapore.

Many countries and local governments have begun funding programs that supply sterile needles to people who inject illegal drugs in an attempt to reduce these contingent risks and especially the contraction and spread of blood-borne diseases. The Drug Policy Alliance reports that up to 75% of new AIDS cases among women and children are directly or indirectly a consequence of drug use by injection. The United States federal government does not operate needle exchanges, although some state and local governments do support needle exchange programs.

Anthropologists Philippe Bourgois and Jeff Schonberg, who did a decade of field work among homeless heroin and crack addicts in San

Francisco, reported that the African-American addicts they observed were more inclined to "direct deposit" heroin into a vein, rather than "skin-popping" their injections. (Skin-popping was a far more widespread practice among the white addicts: "By the midpoint of our fieldwork, most of the whites had given up searching for operable veins and skin-popped. They sank their needles perfunctorily, often through their clothing, into their fatty tissue").

Bourgois and Schonberg describes how the cultural difference between the African-Americans and the whites leads to this contrasting behavior, and also points out that the two different ways to inject heroin comes with different health risks. Skin-popping more often results in abscesses, and direct injection more often leads to fatal overdose and also to hepatitis C and HIV infection.

A heroin overdose is usually treated with an opioid antagonist, such as naloxone (Narcan), or naltrexone, which has high affinity for opioid receptors but does not activate them. This reverses the effects of heroin and other opioid agonists and causes an immediate return of consciousness but may precipitate withdrawal symptoms. The half-life of naloxone is much shorter than that of most opioid agonists, so that antagonist typically has to be administered multiple times until the opioid has been metabolized by the body.

Depending on drug interactions and numerous other factors, death from overdose can take anywhere from several minutes to several hours due to anoxia because the breathing reflex is suppressed by μ-opioids. An overdose is immediately reversible with an opioid antagonist injection. Heroin overdoses can occur due to an unexpected increase in the dose or purity or due to diminished opioid tolerance. However, many fatalities reported as overdoses are probably caused by interactions with other depressant drugs like alcohol or benzodiazepines. It should also be noted that since heroin can cause nausea and vomiting, a significant number of deaths attributed to heroin overdose are caused by aspiration of vomit by an unconscious victim.

Some sources give a figure of between 75 and 375 mg for a 75 kg being fatal for 50% of opiate naive people. Street heroin is of widely varying and unpredictable purity. This means that the user may prepare what they consider to be a moderate dose while actually taking far more than intended. Also, tolerance typically decreases after a period of abstinence. If this occurs and the user takes a dose comparable to their previous use, the user may experience drug effects that are much greater than expected, potentially resulting in a dangerous overdose.

It has been speculated that an unknown portion of heroin related deaths are the result of an overdose or allergic reaction to quinine, which may sometimes be used as a cutting agent.

A final factor contributing to overdoses is place conditioning. Heroin use is a highly ritualized behavior. While the mechanism has yet to be clearly elucidated, longtime heroin users display increased tolerance to the drug in locations where they have repeatedly administered heroin. When the user injects in a different location, this environment-conditioned tolerance does not occur, resulting in a greater drug effect. The user's typical dose of the drug, in the face of decreased tolerance, becomes far too high and can be toxic, leading to overdose.

A small percentage of heroin smokers and occasionally IV users may develop symptoms of toxic leukoencephalopathy. The cause has yet to be identified, but one speculation is that the disorder is caused by an uncommon adulterant that is only active when heated. Symptoms include slurred speech and difficulty walking.

Cocaine sometimes proves to be fatal when used in combination with heroin. Though "speedballs" (when injected) or "moonrocks" (when smoked) are a popular mix of the two drugs among users, combinations of stimulants and depressants can have unpredictable and sometimes fatal results.

In the United States in early 2006, a rash of deaths was attributed to either a combination of fentanyl and heroin, or pure fentanyl masquerading as heroin particularly in the Detroit Metro Area; one news report refers to the combination as 'laced heroin', though this is likely a generic rather than a specific term.

Methamphetamine

Methamphetamine, also known as metamfetamine (INN), dextromethamphetamine, methylamphetamine, N-methylamphetamine, and desoxyephedrine, is a psychoactive stimulant drug. It increases alertness and energy, and in high doses, can induce euphoria, enhance self-esteem, and increase sexual pleasure. Methamphetamine has high potential for abuse, activating the physiological reward system by increasing levels of dopamine and norepinephrine in the brain. Methamphetamine is FDA approved for the treatment of ADHD and exogenous obesity.

Methamphetamine was first synthesized from ephedrine in Japan in 1893 by chemist Nagayoshi Nagai. In 1919, crystallized methamphetamine was synthesized by Akira Ogata via reduction of ephedrine using red phosphorus and iodine. In 1943, Abbott Laboratories requested approval for from the U.S. Food and Drug Administration (FDA) for the treatment of narcolepsy, mild depression, postencephalitic parkinsonism, chronic alcoholism, cerebral arteriosclerosis, and hay fever.

Methamphetamine was approved for all of these indications in December, 1944. All of these indication approvals were eventually removed. The only two approved marketing indications remaining for methamphetamine are for ADHD and the short-term management of exogenous obesity, although the drug is clinically established as effective in the treatment of narcolepsy.

One of the earliest uses of methamphetamine was during World War II when it was used by both Allied and Axis forces. The German military dispensed it under the trade name Pervitin. It was widely distributed across rank and division, from elite forces to tank crews and aircraft personnel, with many millions of tablets being distributed throughout the war.

From 1942 until his death in 1945, Adolf Hitler may have been given intravenous injections of methamphetamine by his personal physician Theodor Morell. It is possible that it was used to treat Hitler's speculated Parkinson's disease, or that his Parkinson-like symptoms that developed from 1940 onwards resulted from using methamphetamine.

After World War II, a large supply of amphetamine stockpiled by the Japanese military became available in Japan under the street name shabu (also Philopon, pronounced Hiropon, a tradename). The Japanese Ministry of Health banned it in 1951; since then it has been increasingly produced by the Yakuza criminal organization. Today methamphetamine is still associated with the Japanese underworld, and its use is discouraged by strong social taboos.

In the 1950s, there was a rise in the legal prescription of methamphetamine to the American public. In the 1954 edition of Pharmacology and Therapeutics, indications for methamphetamine included "narcolepsy, postencephalitic parkinsonism, alcoholism, ... certain depressive states ... and in the treatment of obesity."

The 1960s saw the start of significant use of clandestinely manufactured methamphetamine as well as methamphetamine created in users' own homes for personal use. The recreational use of methamphetamine continues to this day. San Diego, California was described as the "methamphetamine capital of North America" in the December 2, 1989 edition of The Economist and again in 2000, also with South Gate, California as the second capital city.

In 1983, laws were passed in the United States prohibiting possession of precursors and equipment for methamphetamine production; this was followed a month later by a bill passed in Canada enacting similar laws. In 1986, the U.S. government passed the Federal Controlled Substance Analogue Enforcement Act in an attempt to curb the growing use of designer drugs. Despite this, use of methamphetamine expanded throughout rural United States, especially through the Midwest and South.

Since 1989, five U.S. federal laws and dozens of state laws have been imposed in an attempt to curb the production of methamphetamine. Methamphetamine can be produced in home laboratories using pseudoephedrine or ephedrine, which at the time were the active ingredients in over-the-counter drugs such as Sudafed and Contac. Preventative legal strategies of the past 17 years have steadily increased restrictions to the distribution of pseudoephedrine/ephedrine-containing products.

As a result of the U.S. Combat Methamphetamine Epidemic Act of 2005, a subsection of the PATRIOT Act, there are restrictions on the amount of pseudoephedrine and ephedrine one may purchase in a specified time period, and further requirements that these products must be stored in order to prevent theft. Increasingly strict restrictions have resulted in the reformulation of many over-the-counter drugs, and some such as Actifed have been discontinued entirely in the United States.

Physical effects can include anorexia, hyperactivity, dilated pupils, flushing, restlessness, dry mouth, headache, tachycardia, bradycardia, tachypnea, hypertension, hypotension, hyperthermia, diaphoresis, diarrhea, constipation, blurred vision, dizziness, twitching, insomnia, numbness, palpitations, arrhythmias, tremors, dry and/or itchy skin, acne, pallor, and with chronic and/or high dosages, convulsions, heart attack, stroke, and death can occur.

Psychological effects can include euphoria, anxiety, increased libido, alertness, concentration, energy, self-esteem, self-confidence, sociability, irritability, aggression, psychosomatic disorders, psycho-motor agitation, hubris, excessive feelings of power and superiority, repetitive and obsessive behaviors, paranoia, and with chronic and/or high doses, amphetamine psychosis can occur.

As with other amphetamines, tolerance to methamphetamine is not completely understood, but known to be sufficiently complex that it cannot be explained by any single mechanism. The extent of tolerance and the rate at which it develops vary widely between individuals, and even within one person it is highly dependent on dosage, duration of use, and frequency of administration. Tolerance to the awakening effect of amphetamines does not readily develop, making them suitable for the treatment of narcolepsy.

Short-term tolerance can be caused by depleted levels of neurotransmitters within the synaptic vesicles available for release into the synaptic cleft following subsequent reuse (tachyphylaxis). Short-term tolerance typically lasts until neurotransmitter levels are fully replenished; because of the toxic effects on dopaminergic neurons, this can be greater than 2-3 days. Prolonged overstimulation of dopamine receptors caused by methamphetamine may eventually cause the receptors to downregulate in order to compensate for increased levels of dopamine within the synaptic cleft. To compensate, larger quantities of the drug are needed in order to achieve the same level of effects.

Reverse tolerance or sensitization can also occur. The effect is well established but the mechanism is not well understood.

Methamphetamine is addictive. While not dangerous, withdrawal symptoms are common with heavy use and relapse is common. Various organizations, such as Crystal Meth Anonymous, are available to combat relapse.

Methamphetamine-induced hyperstimulation of pleasure pathways leads to anhedonia. It is possible that daily administration of the amino acids L-Tyrosine and L-5HTP/Tryptophan can aid in the recovery process by making it easier for the body to reverse the depletion of dopamine, norepinephrine, and serotonin. Although studies involving the use of these amino acids have shown some success, this method of recovery has not been shown to be consistently effective.

It is shown that taking ascorbic acid prior to using methamphetamine may help reduce acute toxicity to the brain, as rats given the human equivalent of 5-10 grams of ascorbic acid 30 minutes prior to methamphetamine dosage had toxicity mediated, yet this will likely be of little avail in solving the other serious behavioral problems associated with methamphetamine use and addiction that many users experience. Large doses of ascorbic acid also lower urinary pH, reducing methamphetamine's elimination half-life and thus decreasing the duration of its actions.

To combat addiction, doctors are beginning to use other forms of amphetamine such as dextroamphetamine to break the addiction cycle in a method similar to the use of methadone in the treatment of heroin addicts. There are no publicly available drugs comparable to naloxone, which blocks opiate receptors and is therefore used in treating opiate dependence, for use with methamphetamine problems. However, experiments with some monoamine reuptake inhibitors such as indatraline have been successful in blocking the action of methamphetamine. There are studies indicating that fluoxetine, bupropion and imipramine may reduce craving and improve adherence to treatment. Research has also suggested that modafinil can help addicts quit methamphetamine use.

Methamphetamine addiction is one of the most difficult forms of addictions to treat. Bupropion, aripiprazole, and baclofen have been employed to treat post-withdrawal cravings, although the success rate is low. Modafinil is somewhat more successful, but this is a Class IV scheduled drug. Ibogaine has been used with success in Europe, but is a Class I drug and available only for research use. Mirtazapine has been reported useful in some small-population studies

Since the phenethylamine phentermine is a constitutional isomer of methamphetamine, it has been speculated that it may be effective in treating methamphetamine addiction. Phentermine is a central nervous system stimulant that acts on dopamine and norepinephrine, it has not been reported to cause the same degree of euphoria that is associated with other amphetamines.

Abrupt interruption of chronic methamphetamine use results in the withdrawal syndrome in almost 90% of the cases.

The mental depression associated with methamphetamine withdrawal is longer lasting and more severe than that of cocaine withdrawal.

Methamphetamine users and addicts may lose their teeth abnormally quickly, a condition known as "meth mouth". This effect is not caused by any corrosive effects of the drug itself, which is a common myth. According to the American Dental Association, meth mouth "is probably caused by a combination of drug-induced psychological and physiological changes resulting in xerostomia (dry mouth), extended periods of poor oral hygiene, frequent consumption of high-calorie, carbonated beverages and bruxism (teeth grinding and clenching)."Similar, though far less severe symptoms have been reported in clinical use of other amphetamines, where effects are not exacerbated by a lack of oral hygiene for extended periods".

Like other substances that stimulate the sympathetic nervous system, methamphetamine causes decreased production of acid-fighting saliva and increased thirst, resulting in increased risk for tooth decay, especially when thirst is quenched by high-sugar drinks.

Serious health and appearance problems can be caused by unsterilized needles, lack or ignoring of hygiene needs (more typical on chronic use), and obsessive skin-picking, which may lead to abscesses.

Users may exhibit sexually compulsive behavior while under the influence of methamphetamine. This disregard for the potential dangers of unprotected sex or other reckless sexual behavior may contribute to the spread of sexually transmitted infections (STIs) or sexually transmitted diseases (STDs). Among the effects reported by methamphetamine users are increased libido and sexual pleasure, the ability to have sex for extended periods of time, and an inability to ejaculate or reach orgasm. In addition to increasing the need for sex and enabling the user to engage in prolonged sexual activity, methamphetamine lowers inhibitions and may cause users to behave recklessly or to become forgetful.

According to a recent San Diego study, methamphetamine users often engage in unsafe sexual activities, and forget or choose not to use condoms. The study found that methamphetamine users were six times less likely to use condoms. The urgency for sex combined with the inability to achieve physical release (ejaculation) can result in tearing, chafing, and trauma (such as rawness and friction sores) to the sex organs, the rectum and mouth, dramatically increasing the risk of infectious transmission. Methamphetamine also causes erectile dysfunction due to vasoconstriction.

It has been found that the volatile remain products and even the methamphetamine itself can contaminate the "home" methamphetamine labs, thus becoming these places a public health hazard due to the possible consequences for new inhabitants, especially through the respiratory and conjunctiva mucosa, blood stream and Central Nervous System.

Studies have shown that the subjective pleasure of drug use, or the reinforcing component of addiction, is proportional to the rate at which the blood level of the drug increases. In general, intravenous injection is the fastest mechanism, followed by smoking, suppository (anal insertion), insufflation (snorting), and ingestion (swallowing). Ingestion does not produce a rush, which is the most transcendent state of euphoria experienced with the use of methamphetamine, and is the most prominent with intravenous use.

While the onset of the rush produced by injection or smoking can occur in as little as a few seconds, the oral route of administration usually requires approximately half an hour before the high sets in. Thus, oral routes of administration are generally used by recreational or medicinal consumers of the drug, while other more fast-acting routes of administration are used by addicts.

Injection is a popular method for use, also known as slamming, but carries quite serious risks. The hydrochloride salt of methamphetamine is soluble in water; intravenous users may use any dose range from less than 100 milligrams to over one gram using a hypodermic needle (although it should be noted that typically street methamphetamine is "cut" with a water-soluble cutting material, which constitutes a significant portion of a given street methamphetamine dose). Intravenous users often experience skin rashes (sometimes called "speed bumps") and infections at the site of injection. As with the injection of any drug, if a group of users share a common needle or any type of injecting equipment without sterilization procedures, blood-borne diseases such as HIV or hepatitis can be transmitted.

"Smoking" amphetamines refers to vaporizing it to inhale the resulting fumes, not burning it to inhale the resulting smoke. It is commonly smoked in glass pipes made from blown Pyrex tubes, light bulbs, or on aluminum foil heated underneath by a flame. This method is also known as "chasing the white dragon" (whereas smoking heroin is known as "chasing the dragon"). There is little evidence that methamphetamine inhalation results in greater toxicity than any other route of administration. Lung damage has been reported with long-term use, but manifests in forms independent of route (pulmonary hypertension and associated complications), or limited to injection users (pulmonary emboli).

Another popular route to intake methamphetamine is insufflation (snorting), where a user crushes the methamphetamine into a fine powder and then sharply inhales it (sometimes with a straw or a rolled up banknote similar to cocaine) into the nose where methamphetamine is absorbed through the soft tissue in the mucous membrane of the sinus cavity straight into the bloodstream. This method bypasses first pass metabolism and has a quicker onset with a higher bioavailability, although the duration is shorter than with oral administration. This method is sometimes preferred by users who do not want to prepare and administer methamphetamine for injection or smoking, but still experience a fast onset with a rush.

Methamphetamine is most structurally similar to methcathinone and amphetamine. When illicitly produced, it is commonly made by the reduction of ephedrine or pseudoephedrine. Most of the necessary chemicals are readily available in household products or over-the-counter cold or allergy medicines. Synthesis is relatively simple, but entails risk with flammable and corrosive chemicals, particularly the solvents used in extraction and purification. Clandestine production is therefore often discovered by fires and explosions caused by the improper handling of volatile or flammable solvents.

Most methods of illicit production involve hydrogenation of the hydroxyl group on the ephedrine or pseudoephedrine molecule. The most common method for small-scale methamphetamine labs in the United States is primarily called the "Red, White, and Blue Process", which involves red phosphorus, pseudoephedrine or ephedrine (white), and blue iodine (which is technically a purple color in elemental form), from which hydroiodic acid is formed.

In Australia, criminal groups have been known to substitute "red" phosphorus with either hypophosphorous acid or phosphorous acid. This is a fairly dangerous process for amateur chemists, because phosphine gas, a side-product from in situ hydroiodic acid production, is extremely toxic to inhale.

Another common method uses the Birch reduction (also called the "Nagai method"), in which metallic lithium, commonly extracted from non-rechargeable lithium batteries, is substituted for difficult-to-find metallic sodium. However, the Birch reduction is dangerous because the alkali metal and liquid anhydrous ammonia are both extremely reactive, and the temperature of liquid ammonia makes it susceptible to explosive boiling when reactants are added. Anhydrous ammonia and lithium or sodium (Birch reduction) may be surpassing hydroiodic acid (catalytic hydrogenation) as the most common method of manufacturing methamphetamine in the U.S. and possibly in Mexico. New Jersey as well as Maine both rank in the top illegal underground methamphetamine producing states.

A completely different procedure of synthesis uses the reductive amination of phenylacetone with methylamine, both of which are currently DEA list I chemicals (as are pseudoephedrine and ephedrine). The reaction requires a catalyst that acts as a reducing agent, such as mercury-aluminum amalgam or platinum dioxide, also known as Adams' catalyst. This was once the preferred method of production by motorcycle gangs in California, until DEA restrictions on the chemicals made the process difficult. Other less common methods use other means of hydrogenation, such as hydrogen gas in the presence of a catalyst.

Methamphetamine labs can give off noxious fumes, such as phosphine gas, methylamine gas, solvent vapors; such as acetone or chloroform, iodine vapors, white phosphorus, anhydrous ammonia, hydrogen chloride/muriatic acid, hydrogen iodide, lithium/sodium metal, ether, or methamphetamine vapors. If performed by amateurs, manufacturing methamphetamine can be extremely dangerous. If the red phosphorus overheats, because of a lack of ventilation, phosphine gas can be produced. This gas is highly toxic and if present in large quantities is likely to explode upon autoignition from diphosphine, which is formed by overheating phosphorus.

In recent years, reports of a simplified "Shake 'n Bake" synthesis have surfaced. The method is suitable for such small batches that pseudoephedrine restrictions are less effective, it uses chemicals that are easier to obtain, though no less dangerous than traditional methods, and it is so easy to carry out that some addicts have made the drug while driving. Producing meth in this fashion can be extremely dangerous and has been linked to several fatalities.

Temazepam

Temazepam is commonly marketed under brand names Normison, Temtabs, Euhypnos, Restoril, Remestan, Tenox and Norkotral. It is an intermediate-acting 3-hydroxy benzodiazepine. Temazepam is generally prescribed for the short-term treatment of sleeplessness in patients who have difficulty maintaining sleep. In addition, temazepam has anti-anxiety, anticonvulsant, and skeletal muscle relaxant properties.

Temazepam was first synthesized in 1964, but it first came into use in 1969 when its ability to counter insomnia was realized. By the late 1980s, temazepam was one of the most popular and widely prescribed hypnotics on the market and it became one of the most widely prescribed drugs.

Temazepam is a hypnotic agent. In sleep laboratory studies, temazepam significantly decreased the number of nightly awakenings but has the drawback of distorting the normal sleep pattern. The drug is officially indicated for severe insomnia and other severe or disabling sleep disorders. The prescribing guidelines limit prescribing of hypnotics to two-to-four weeks due to concerns of tolerance and dependence.

The United States Air Force uses temazepam as one of the hypnotics approved as "no-go pills" to help aviators and special duty personnel sleep in support of mission readiness. "Ground tests" are required prior to authorization being issued to use the medication in an operational situation.

Temazepam should not be used in pregnancy, as it may cause harm to the fetus. The safety and effectiveness of temazepam has not been established in children. Therefore temazepam should generally not be given to individuals under 18 years of age, and should not be used at all in children under 6 months old. Benzodiazepines also require special caution if used in the elderly, alcohol or drug-dependent individuals and individuals with comorbid psychiatric disorders.

The smallest possible effective dose should be used in elderly or very ill patients, as there is a risk of apnea and/or cardiac arrest. This risk is increased when temazepam is given concomitantly with other drugs that depress the central nervous system.

Since benzodiazepines can be abused and lead to dependence, their use should be avoided in people in certain particularly high risk groups. High risk groups include people with a history of alcohol or drug abuse or dependence, emotionally unstable patients, people with severe personality disorders, such as Borderline Personality Disorder. If temazepam is indeed prescribed to people in these groups, they should generally be monitored very closely for signs of abuse and development of dependence.

Side effects typical of hypnotic benzodiazepines are related to CNS depression, and include somnolence, dizziness, fatigue, ataxia, headache, lethargy, impairment of memory and learning, increased reaction time and impairment of motor functions, coordination problems, slurred speech, decreased physical performance, numbed emotions, reduced alertness, muscle weakness, blurred vision, and inattention. Euphoria was rarely reported with the use of temazepam. According to the FDA, temazepam had an incidence of euphoria of 1.5%, much more rarely reported than headaches and diarrhea. Anterograde amnesia may also develop, as may respiratory depression in higher doses.

Hyperhydrosis, hypotension, burning eyes, changes in libido, hallucinations, faintness, nystagmus, vomiting, pruritus, gastrointestinal disturbances, nightmares, palpitation and paradoxical reactions including restlessness, aggression, violence, overstimulation and agitation have been reported, but are rare.

Before taking temazepam, one should ensure that at least 8 hours are available to dedicate to sleep. Failing to do so can increase the side effects of the drug.

The use of this drug in combination with alcohol potentiates the side effects, and can lead to toxicity and death.

Though rare, residual "hangover" effects after nighttime administration of temazepam such as sleepiness, impaired psychomotor and cognitive functions may persist into the next day, which may impair the ability of users to drive safely or may increase the risks of falls and hip fractures.

Chronic or excessive use of temazepam may cause drug tolerance, which can develop rapidly, so this drug is therefore not recommended for long-term use. In 1979 the Institute of Medicine and the National Institute on Drug Abuse stated that most hypnotics lose their sleep-inducing properties after about 3 to 14 days. In use longer than 1-2 weeks, tolerance will frequently develop towards the ability of temazepam to maintain sleep, so that the drug loses effectiveness. Some studies have observed tolerance to temazepam after as little as one week's use.

Another study examined the short-term effects of the accumulation of temazepam over 7 days in elderly inpatients, and found that little tolerance developed during the accumulation of the drug. Other studies examined the use of temazepam over six days and saw no evidence of tolerance. A study in 11 young male subjects showed that significant tolerance occurs to temazepam's thermoregulatory effects and sleep inducing properties after 1 week of use of 30 mg temazepam. Body temperature is well correlated with the sleep inducing or insomnia promoting properties of drugs.

In one study the drug sensitivity of people who had used temazepam for 1-20 years was no different from that of controls. An additional study, in which at least one of the authors is employed by multiple drug companies, examined the efficacy of temazepam treatment on chronic insomnia over three months and saw no drug tolerance, with the authors even suggesting that the drug might become more effective over time.

Temazepam like other benzodiazepine drugs can cause physical dependence and addiction. Withdrawal from temazepam or other benzodiazepines after regular use often leads to a benzodiazepine withdrawal syndrome, which resembles symptoms during alcohol and barbiturate withdrawal. The higher the dose and the longer the drug is taken for, the greater the risk of experiencing unpleasant withdrawal symptoms. Withdrawal symptoms can also occur from standard dosages and after short term use. Abrupt withdrawal from therapeutic doses of temazepam after long term use may result in a severe benzodiazepine withdrawal syndrome. Gradual and careful reduction of the dosage, preferably with a long-acting benzodiazepine with long half life active metabolites such as chlordiazepoxide or diazepam is recommended, to prevent severe withdrawal syndromes from developing. Other hypnotic benzodiazepines are not recommended.

A study in rats found that temazepam is cross tolerant with barbiturates and is able to effectively substitute for barbiturates and suppress barbiturate withdrawal signs. There are rare reports in the medical literature of psychotic states developing after abrupt withdrawal from benzodiazepines, even from therapeutic doses. Antipsychotics increase the severity of benzodiazepine withdrawal effects with an increase in the intensity and severity of convulsions. Patients who were treated in the hospital with temazepam or nitrazepam have continued taking these after leaving the hospital. It was recommended that hypnotics in the hospital be limited to 5 nights use only, to avoid the development of withdrawal symptoms like insomnia.

Temazepam is a drug with the potential for misuse. Drug misuse is defined as taking the drug to achieve a high, or continuing to take the drug in the long term against medical advice.

In North America, temazepam abuse is not widespread. Other benzodiazepines are more commonly prescribed for insomnia. In the United States, temazepam is the fifth most prescribed benzodiazepine. Individuals abusing benzodiazepines obtain the drug by getting prescriptions from several doctors, forging prescriptions, or buying diverted pharmaceutical products on the illicit market. North America never had a serious problem with temazepam abuse, but is becoming increasingly vulnerable to the illicit trade of temazepam.

Street terms for temazepam include king kong pills (formerly referred to barbiturates, now more commonly refers to temazepam), jellies, jelly, Edinburgh eccies, tams, terms, mazzies, temazies, tammies, temmies, beans, eggs, green eggs, wobbly eggs, knockouts, hardball, norries, oranges, rugby balls, ruggers, terminators, red and blue, no-gos, blackout, green devils, drunk pills, brainwash, mind erasers, tem-tem's (combined with buprenorphine), mommy's big helper, vitamin T, big T, TZ, and others.

Nootropic

Nootropics, also referred to as smart drugs, memory enhancers, and cognitive enhancers, are drugs, supplements, nutraceuticals, and functional foods that are purported to improve mental functions such as cognition, memory, intelligence, motivation, attention, and concentration. The word nootropic was coined in 1964 by the Romanian Dr. Corneliu E. Giurgea, derived from the Greek words nous, or "mind," and trepein meaning "to bend/turn". Nootropics are thought to work by altering the availability of the brain's supply of neurochemicals (neurotransmitters, enzymes, and hormones), by improving the brain's oxygen supply, or by stimulating nerve growth. However the efficacy of nootropic substances, in most cases, has not been conclusively determined. This is complicated by the difficulty of defining and quantifying cognition and intelligence.

At present, there are several drugs on the market that improve memory, concentration, planning, and reduce impulsive behavior. Many more are in different stages of development. The most commonly used class of drug are the stimulants.

These drugs are used primarily to treat people with cognitive difficulties: Alzheimer's disease, Parkinson's disease, ADHD. However, more widespread use is being recommended by some researchers. These drugs have a variety of human enhancement applications as well, and are marketed heavily on the internet. Nevertheless, intense marketing may not correlate with efficacy; while scientific studies support some of the claimed benefits, it is worth noting that many of the claims attributed to most nootropics have not been formally tested.

In academia, modafinil has been used to increase productivity, although its long-term effects have not been assessed in healthy individuals. Stimulants such as methylphenidate and atomoxetine are being used on college campuses, and by an increasingly younger group. One survey found that 7% of students had used stimulants for a cognitive edge in the past year, and on some campuses the number is as high as 25%.

* * *

Cognitive function is largely impacted by one's diet. The nutrients in food can influence our memory, learning, concentration, and decision-making. Therefore the lack of them has a negative effect on the brain. So far, the studies have been able to link brain function to vitamin B1 and B12, omega-3, caffeine, antioxidants, protein, and iron. In addition, there is research on certain supplements and whether or not they have any benefit, and how blood glucose levels play an effect on concentration and recall.

Vitamin B is vital in cognitive function, but not all B vitamins play a role in brain function. Some aid in the synthesis of chemicals, but two in particular have a significant influence in brain function. Vitamin B1, thiamin, aids nerve cell function and helps the body convert food, specifically carbohydrates, into fuel known as glucose. Glucose is what the brain uses as an energy source, making it a very critical need for the brain.

Foods containing vitamin B1 include whole grains, rice, wheat germ, bran and organ meats. Vitamin B12, cobalamin, is used to make neurotransmitters. One of their primary functions is the formation of blood cells. They also maintain the nervous system by helping to metabolize fatty acids, which are essential for the maintenance of myelin that surrounds nerves. Vitamin B12 is found primarily in animal products, but it may also be found in eggs, seaweeds and algae. In addition to including vitamin B in one's diet, there are factors that can play a role in the uptake and use of vitamin B.

Homocysteine and folate each affect how various vitamin B's are metabolized. Homocysteine is a byproduct of the body's metabolism of methionine, one of the essential amino acids, although not one used to build protein that is converted back to methionine or cysteine, through reactions with certain B vitamins. Methionine is used to breakdown fats, which is crucial, since the brain needs certain fats to function properly. Cysteine helps to detoxify harmful substances in the body and can also help to increase levels of the antioxidant glutathione, a substance which helps to stop compounds in the body that alter cell membranes, tamper with DNA, or cause cell death.

In one of many studies young mice genetically predisposed to atherosclerosis were fed one of four diets for 8 weeks, which differed in B vitamin and methionine contents. Psychomotor, memory, spatial and learning tests were done, and researchers reported brain dysfunction in those with low vitamin B intake. Low amounts of vitamin B12 with normal folate have been shown to cause cognitive impairment and anemia, while high amounts of folate and normal vitamin B12 have been shown to improve cognitive function. While vitamin B1 and B12 improve cognitive function, it is not enough; other dietary factors come into play as well.

Omega-3, or alpha linolenic acid, has a strong influence on the brain. It influences both communication between cells and cell function. It appears to make receptors on the cell membranes that are more sensitive to serotonin, a neurotransmitter, which helps give us a "happy" feeling. Omega-3 has also been linked to helping retain brain function. A study done in Norway, proved how omega-3 eaten during pregnancy helped to produce a more intelligent child. Increasing omega-3 in the diet has been shown to lower risk of depression, even better than depression medication.

Omega - 3's are what build cell membranes. Omega-3's can be found in cold-water fish, such as salmon, as well as almonds, avocadoes, walnuts and flaxseed. Fish oils in particular, are components of nerve cell membranes and myelin, which help to keep blood vessels in the brain healthy. A study on cats demonstrated that fish oil reduced the degree of brain damage experienced in cerebral stroke. Unfortunately today, it is harder to find regular sources of omega-3.

Interestingly enough, diets of prehistoric families included sufficient amounts of omega-3 due to cooking methods and agricultural practices, yet in today's world such practices are no longer the norm. Traditional sources of omega-3 could be found richly in cattle, since they used to graze on grass, which contains omega-3, but today they are mostly fed grain, which does not contain omega-3's. Today's society gets a bit too much omega-6, and less of omega-3, both of which are polyunsaturated fats.

While unsaturated fats, such as omega-3 fat, are known to be beneficial to the brain, saturated fats, are not. According to the Sukitt-Hale, saturated fat, which is a triglyceride, is strongly linked to causing depression, manic depression and schizoaffective disorder, in addition to hostility and aggression. Studies on patients have showed that lowering levels of triglycerides help to alleviate depression and improve scores on dementia screening tests in the elderly.

One cause for this is due to the fact that high levels of triglycerides increase blood sluggishness, so it becomes harder for the blood to transport sufficient amounts of oxygen to brain cells. Without oxygen in the brain, mini brain lesions and blood clots can form. Memory tests have also been done on rats that were fed high saturated fat diets and found those with the least amount of saturated and total fat to have performed better in the memory tests.

A study done on infant rhesus monkeys lead by William Connor, M.D, also concurred with these results when they fed each monkey diets with adequate amounts of fat, but differed in the types of fats. The ones with more saturated fats grew well, but their visual development was impaired and they kept pacing and forth, as if they had a neurological defect, while the ones with unsaturated fats grew normally. Although, one must keep in mind that not all omega-3's are made the same. Long-chain omega-3's appear to be more favorable in the brain, compared to the medium lengths, which are found in plants.

There are many mixed opinions about caffeine and the effects that it has on the brain. Some say that it helps cognitive function, while others find its benefits to be equivalent to its negative effects. Caffeine reaches its highest concentration in the blood and brain within 30-40 minutes after consumption and does not build up in the body, due to excretion, although it may take around 12 hours to completely leave the body and even longer in smokers or pregnant women. It has been shown to increase alertness, performance and in some studies memory.

Children and adults who consume low doses of caffeine showed increase alertness, yet a higher dose was needed to improve performance. A 2007 study found that caffeinated beverages seem to help improve short-term concentration and facilitate learning, as well as memory. Caffeine dilates the blood vessels in the brain, if consumed in small amounts. Scientists compared the benefits and effects of coffee versus tea. Coffee took effect within 20 minutes and lasted for 2-3 hours, while tea, had a weaker effect, yet lasted longer, since it was released more slowly, although, the scientists emphasized moderation, since some studies suggested that too much caffeine would decrease concentration.

One underlining factor, is also the liquid in caffeinated beverages, which helps to stabilize circulation and nutrient transport. Negative effects of caffeine are not seen if it is consumed 6 hours or more apart and in appropriate doses. Such regular consumption may also enhance the neuro-protective actions of adenosine. Adenosine is a nucleoside that contains adenine as its base. Adenosine dilates the coronary arteries and is employed in the adenosine thallium scan of heart. Caffeine has also been shown to have more of an effect on improving cognitive performance and sustaining attention in older adults. Chronic pretreatment of caffeine in animals has shown to reduce ischaemic brain damage, in addition to reducing the risk of Parkinson's disease. Although, caffeine may help brain function, it may not necessarily be recommended for those who do not already consume it.

Those opposed to caffeine, find there to be little to no acute benefit from regular caffeine consumption due to withdrawal lowering alertness and mood. After consumption, it is rapidly distributed throughout the body and blocks actions of endogenous adenosine at adenosine A1 and A2 receptors resulting in different physiological effects. The blockage is how caffeine can affect alertness and performance, since adenosine is closely involved in sleep regulation. For example, the extra cellular adenosine concentration increases during waking and decreases during sleep.

Withdrawal from caffeine tends to cause headaches, with its increase in cerebral blood flow. It is worse for those who typically consume caffeine and then try to abstain from it for a long term. There was no shown effect on performance in non-consumers and long-term withdrawn consumers, even when sleep deprived. Still, such findings may be due to the fact that those who were studied who did not consume caffeine were different in that they already functioned well without caffeine, so they had no need or was not missing any gap to begin with.

Another problem with caffeine is that it causes an anxiety and jitteriness effect, although some heath surveys have found caffeine to improve mood in both young and old adults. It is thought that depression, stress and anxiety, may be lessened with caffeine. Beverages that contain caffeine typically have antioxidants as well, which have show to have a strong association with improving brain cognition.

Antioxidants have been found to be very beneficial to brain functioning in many ways. The more commonly known aspect of antioxidants on the brain would be their protection from oxidative damage. A study which lasted 3-6 years, showed how vegetables, most likely due to their vitamin E, folate and antioxidant content, helped people to retain their mental abilities longer, keeping their brain younger. Those vegetables emphasized were leafy green or cruciferous vegetables. Both polyphenolics and isoflavones are two types of antioxidants that have been studied.

Polyphenolics, also known as phenols, in fruits and vegetables may help brain functioning. The darker colored fruits and vegetables tend to be high in phenolics, therefore possessing large antioxidant and inflammatory activity. At high levels, it has been shown that these effects can retard and reverse bits of brain aging, such as dopamine release and other cognitive deficits. The polyphenolics increased antioxidant and anti-inflammatory levels. Such effects are particularly effective with dietary intake of berry fruit.

A study was done on rats, where a 2% blackberry supplemented diet was shown effective in reversing age related deficits and neural function. This diet helped improve motor performance based on three tasks. Polyphenolics positively affect brain signaling to enhance neural communication. In addition to polyphenolics, falvonoids and other antioxidants also help to get rid of free radicals.

Other antioxidants include flavoniods, tannins, pheolic acids and stillbenoids. Berries are a great antioxidant food source, and happen to be high in flavonoids, condensed and hydrolysable tannins, phenolic acids and stillbenoids, amongst other properties, such as cyanidin-3-O-glucoside, which has the highest oxygen radial absorbance capacity among anthocyanins. Blackberries are high in antiproliferative, antioxidant and anti-inflammatory activities, making them a great food for the brain.

In a study showing the benefits of blackberries, rats were fed a 2% blackberry diet, and they were able to perform much better on behavioral tests than the control rats. According to Nutritional Neuroscience, blackberry juice and its main anthocyanin component, cyaniding-3-O-glucoside had been seen to the protective effect against free radical-mediated endothelial dysfunction and vascular failure. Blackberries, like blueberries, may exert their protective effects directly through alterations in cell signaling to improve or increase neuronal communication, calcium buffering ability, neuroprotective stress shock proteins, and plasticity on stress signaling pathways.

The study had found that the blueberry diet improved spatial working memory in older rats, and changes were regulated by the camp response element binding (CREB) and brain-dervied neurotrophic factor (BDNF) pathway in the hippocampus. Anthocyanins, which are found in blueberries and blackberries, enter the brain and improve cognitive function. Isoflavonoes have been found to help the cognitive process, but in a different way.

A study done in 2008 found that consumption of isoflavonoes of 50 mg of soy dietary supplements twice a day for three weeks, decreased a biomarker of DNA oxidation damage. Isoflavones are a plant derived class of phytoestrogens. They are richest in soy products, but can also be found in foods such as legumes. There is some evidence suggesting that isoflavones may protect the brain from cognitive decline. Scientists reported that the UK the Joint Health believed that soy protein helps to reduce cholesterol, which may impact how the brain works. Another study that looked mainly at the effects of soy on females during their cycle.

This was done because the estrogen levels constantly change throughout the female cycle. The results suggested that, dietary phytoestrogens may have an effect on cognitive function in females and that soy appeared to affect some cognitive processes. While soy products do contain isoflavones, which has shown benefit they also contain many essential amino acids, which may partially explain the benefits of soy other than isoflavones.

Adult brains use amino acids, which are typically found in protein rich food, for the production of enzymes that transport molecules, structural material and neurotransmitters, along with other essential molecules. Some of the amino acids include tyrosine and phenylalanine, which help to produce the hormone epinephrine and neurotransmitter dopamine. These two hormones help create alertness.

Nutrition scientist Karina Fischer and her colleges, suggest eating a high protein, but low calorie meals, to increases alertness and attentiveness, although too much protein can have a negative effect as well. In addition to toxicity, which too high protein levels can cause, foods high in protein tend to have less tryptophan, a precursor to the neurotransmitter serotonin, which could cause tryptophan depletion. Tryptophan helps to stabilize mood and may also influence the cognitive process, specifically learning and memory.

There have been both human and rat studies which have indicated a deficit in long term memory and information processing due to tryptophan depletion and other studies show how tryptophan helps to improve decision making. While foods high in carbohydrates, which do not contain tryptophan, they do help to push tryptophan into the brain, by triggering the release of insulin. Insulin stimulates muscles to take up competing amino acids. Even, calcium, which typically comes in many foods with protein, helps regulate nerve impulse transmission.

Two other important neurotransmitters are acetylcholine and serotonin. Acetylcholine is essential in memory formation and maintenance. It is found in egg yolks and organ meats. Creation and utilization of acetylcholine is crucial to memory. Serotonin helps with sleep regulation and anxiety reduction. It is manufactured from tryptophan. In addition to amino acids, iron is also necessarily for a fully functioning brain.

Iron is also important for staying mentally sharp. It helps create hemoglobin, an iron containing protein in red blood cells, which transport oxygen to the brain. Oxygen in the brain is vital, since it helps to metabolize glucose. If a child does not receive enough iron, it can impair brain development and lead to deficits in speech, math and reading. Women of reproductive age need the most iron, and therefore may be more likely to end up with a deficiency. Those with sufficient iron in their blood have been proven to perform better cognitive tests than those who were iron-deficient. While, we want to aim to get all these nutrients, it is sometimes hard and we may rely on supplements, which can sometimes be beneficial in supporting brain function, depending on the supplement

Typical diets do not contain all our required amounts of nutrients, therefore it is recommended to take supplements and/or daily multi-vitamins. Although we would like for the multivitamin to fill in where we are missing nutrients from the diet, that is not always the case. Some nutrients are absorbed better than others and we do not always receive the same benefit from supplements as we would from the nutrient in real food. Research has examined a few of the supplements for nutrients that have been found to improve cognitive function and have found some to be beneficial, while others showed to have little to no effect.

Some studies found certain supplements to be beneficial only in certain situations. Supplemental tyrosine, epinephrine and norepinephrine, which all play large roles in the brains response to stress, were found only to be beneficial in stressful conditions. In one study, soldiers were exposed to high altitudes or prolonged cold, which would normally deplete the body of tyrosine, due to environmental stress, the soldiers who took the supplement did not suffer the loss of memory or any other side effects such as headache and lightheadedness. The one thing to consider in taking theses amino acid supplements is that they will tend to compete with one another for absorption.

So if too many amino acids are obtained from supplements, it may be counterproductive, since it would probably throw the body off balance, due to only a few being absorbed. Choline, on the other hand, since it is not an amino acid does not have to compete, so supplementation should be fine. While, these work in at least specific conditions, some supplements have been found to have no effect on cognitive function.

There is little evidence of a benefit in terms of cognitive function, from taking B vitamins or antioxidant supplements. Data from a wide variety of trials, found there to be no changes in cognitive function from taking vitamin B supplements in either healthy or cognitively impaired individuals. Yet, such results could be due to insufficient duration of supplementation. It may also be that the trials were done on older adults and vitamin B supplementation effect could be more beneficial at a younger age, when the brain is still developing. Cognitive decline may be very difficult to reverse in older adults. While taking supplements is one alternative to increasing brain function, watching glycemic index is another.

In addition to what you eat, when and how you eat also plays a role in how the brain operates. This is primarily due to the need of constant supply of glucose for the brain. Optimal brainpower is reached when blood glucose is stable. This is where diets, such as trying to eat a low glycemic index, can be beneficial. Simple sugars can spike blood glucose and their glucose supply does not last long, so they should be avoided. Too high blood glucose can also inhibit mental function, according to Cox, who had run cognitive tests on diabetics. Their verbal and math skills were much slower and less actuate when their glucose levels rose too high. It is best to substitute them for complex carbohydrates, fiber rich food, starch whole grains, protein, legumes or vegetables, which take longer to be broken down and therefore, do not spike blood glucose.

Eating regularly and snacking can help maintain glucose supply to the brain. Unfortunately, the brain cannot store carbohydrates, which is why it is in need of a constant supply of glucose. Without it, we loose the ability to concentrate. If one is low on glucose supply due to fasting, the brain is forced to get its energy from metabolizing ketones, which come from the breakdown of body fat, and cognitive function worsens, since it requires synthesis of special enzymes which take longer to metabolize. The saying, "eating breakfast helps one do better in school," is not a wives tale, but truly does help one stay alert, focused and have a better retention rate. Some suggestions for food are to eat fruit and yogurt or whole grain bread and low fat cheese. Surprisingly, even something as little as chewing gum could help improve memory. When picking foods, its is recommended to try to choose foods lower in saturated fats and cholesterol as well as simple sugars.

Choosing a diet with appropriate levels of cholesterol has been shown to be beneficial in terms of brain function, although the specifics are controversial. Diets too low in cholesterol, which some people strive for thinking it helps out their heart, have been linked to increased risk of suicide. Too little cholesterol makes the brain unstable, which tells us that it is clearly missing something in cholesterol that is vital to our brains function. High cholesterol levels are also bad for the brain, especially when they are due to saturated fat. So keeping in mind saturated fat and cholesterol when eating, really does help more than the heart.

Entheogen

An entheogen, in the strict sense, is a psychoactive substance used in a religious, shamanic or spiritual context. Historically, entheogens were mostly derived from plant sources and have been used in a variety of traditional religious contexts. Most entheogens do not produce drug dependency. With the advent of organic chemistry, there now exist many synthetic substances with similar psychoactive properties. Entheogens are tools to supplement various practices for healing and transcendence, including in meditation, psychonautics, art projects, and psychedelic therapy.

More broadly, the term entheogen is used to refer to any psychoactive substances when used for their religious or spiritual effects, whether or not in a formal religious or traditional structure. This terminology is often chosen to contrast with recreational use of the same substances. Spiritual effects of psychedelic compounds have been demonstrated scientifically, or the distinction between these kinds of mind states may be redundant. Research is limited due to drug prohibition.

Examples of traditional entheogens include: Greek: kykeon, ambrosia; African: Iboga; Vedic: Soma, Amrit; Native American: Peyote [North], Ayahuasca [South]. Other traditional entheogens include cannabis. Entheogens have been used in a ritualized context for thousands of years; their religious significance is well established in anthropological and modern evidences. Many pure active compounds with psychoactive properties have been isolated from organisms and chemically synthesized, including mescaline, psilocin/psilocybin, salvinorin A and ibogaine. Entheogens may be compounded through the work of a shaman or apothecary in a tea, admixture, or potion like Ayahuasca/Yage, Bhang, or an anointing oil.

The neologism entheogen was coined in 1979 by a group of ethnobotanists and scholars of mythology that included Carl A. P. Ruck, Jeremy Bigwood, Danny Staples, Richard Evans Schultes, Jonathan Ott and R. Gordon Wasson. The literal meaning of the word is "that which causes God to be within an individual". The translation "creating the divine within" is sometimes given, but entheogen implies neither that something is created nor that that which is experienced is within the user.

The term is derived from two words of ancient Greek,. entheos and genesthai. The adjective entheos translates to English as "full of the god, inspired, possessed," and is the root of the English word "enthusiasm." The Greeks used it as a term of praise for poets and other artists. Genesthai means "to come into being." Thus, an entheogen is a substance that causes one to become inspired or to experience feelings of inspiration, often in a religious or "spiritual" manner.

The word was coined as a replacement for the terms hallucinogen and psychedelic. Hallucinogen was popularized by Aldous Huxley's experiences with mescaline, which were published as The Doors of Perception in 1954. Psychedelic, on the other hand, is a Greek neologism for "mind manifest", and was coined by psychiatrist Humphry Osmond; Aldous Huxley was a volunteer in experiments Osmond was conducting on mescaline.

Some have argued that the term hallucinogen was inappropriate due to its etymological relationship to words relating to delirium and insanity. The term psychedelic was also seen as problematic, due to the similarity in sound to words pertaining to psychosis and also due to the fact that it had become irreversibly associated with various connotations of 1960s pop culture. In modern usage entheogen may be used synonymously with these terms, or it may be chosen to contrast with recreational use of the same substances.

In a strict sense, only those vision-producing drugs that can be shown to have figured in shamanic or religious rites would be designated entheogens, but in a looser sense, the term could also be applied to other drugs, both natural and artificial, that induce alterations of consciousness similar to those documented for ritual ingestion of traditional entheogens.

The use of the word entheogen in its broad sense as a synonym for "hallucinogenic drug" has attracted much criticism.

Notable, early testing of the experience includes the Marsh Chapel Experiment, conducted by physician and theology doctoral candidate, Walter Pahnke, under the supervision of Timothy Leary and the Harvard Psilocybin Project. In this double-blind experiment, volunteer graduate school divinity students from the Boston area almost all claimed to have had profound religious experiences subsequent to the ingestion of pure psilocybin. In 2006, a more rigorously controlled experiment was conducted at Johns Hopkins University, and yielded similar results. To date there is little peer-reviewed research on this subject, due to ongoing drug prohibition and the difficulty of getting approval from institutional review boards.

Archaeologists have proposed several examples of the cultural use of entheogens athat are found in the archaeological record. Evidence for the first use of entheogens may come from Tassili, Algeria, with a cave painting of a mushroom-man, dating to 8000 BP. Hemp seeds discovered by archaeologists at Pazyryk suggest early ceremonial practices by the

Scythians occurred during the 5th to 2nd century BC, confirming previous historical reports by Herodotus.

Essentially all psychoactive drugs that are naturally occurring in plants, fungi, or animals, can be used in an entheogenic context. However, this does not mean they have been used throughout history for religious use.

Although entheogens are taboo and most of them are officially prohibited in Christian and Islamic societies, their ubiquity and prominence in the spiritual traditions of various other cultures is unquestioned. The entheogen, "the spirit, for example, need not be chemical, as is the case with the ivy and the olive: and yet the god was felt to be within them; nor need its possession be considered something detrimental, like drugged, hallucinatory, or delusionary: but possibly instead an invitation to knowledge or whatever good the god's spirit had to offer."

Most of the well-known modern examples, such as peyote, psilocybe and other psychoactive mushrooms, are from the native cultures of the Americas. However, it has also been suggested that entheogens played an important role in ancient Indo-European culture. For , by inclusion in the ritual preparations of the Soma, the "pressed juice" that is the subject of Book 9 of the Rig Veda. Soma was ritually prepared and drunk by priests and initiates and elicited a paean in the Rig Veda that embodies the nature of an entheogen:

"Splendid by Law! declaring Law, truth speaking, truthful in thy works, Enouncing faith, King Soma!... O [Soma] Pavāmana (mind clarifying), place me in that deathless, undecaying world wherein the light of heaven is set, and everlasting lustre shines.... Make me immortal in that realm where happiness and transports, where joy and felicities combine..."

The Kykeon that preceded initiation into the Eleusinian Mysteries is another entheogen, which was investigated (before the word was coined) by Carl Kerényi, in Eleusis: Archetypal Image of Mother and Daughter. Other entheogens in the Ancient Near East and the Aegean include the poppy, Datura, the unidentified "lotus" eaten by the Lotus-Eaters in the Odyssey and Narkissos.

According to some, the familiar shamanic entheogen that the Indo-Europeans brought with them was knowledge of the wild Amanita mushroom. It could not be cultivated; thus it had to be found, which suited it to a nomadic lifestyle. When they reached the world of the Caucasus and the Aegean, the Indo-Europeans encountered wine, the entheogen of Dionysus, who brought it with him from his birthplace in the mythical Nysa, when he returned to claim his Olympian birthright. The Indo-

European proto-Greeks "recognized it as the entheogen of Zeus, and their own traditions of shamanism, the Amanita and the 'pressed juice' of Soma, but better since no longer unpredictable and wild, the way it was found among the Hyperboreans. As befit their own assimilation of agrarian modes of life, the entheogen was now cultivable". Robert Graves, in his foreword to The Greek Myths, hypothesises that the Ambrosia of various pre-Hellenic tribes were amanita, which, based on the morphological similarity of the words amanita, amrita and ambrosia, is entirely plausible, and perhaps panaeolus mushrooms.

Amanita was divine food, and was not something to be indulged in or sampled lightly or something to be profaned. It was the food of the gods, their ambrosia, and it mediated between the two realms. It is said that Tantalus's crime was inviting commoners to share his ambrosia.

The entheogen is believed to offer godlike powers in many traditional tales, including immortality. The failure of Gilgamesh in retrieving the plant of immortality from beneath the waters teaches that the blissful state cannot be taken by force or guile: when Gilgamesh lay on the bank, exhausted from his heroic effort, the serpent came and ate the plant.

Another attempt at subverting the natural order is told in, according to some, a strangely metamorphosed myth, in which natural roles have been reversed to suit the Hellenic world-view. The Alexandrian Apollodorus relates how Gaia (spelled "Ge" in the following passage), Mother Earth herself, has supported the Titans in their battle with the Olympian intruders. The Giants have been defeated:

"When Ge learned of this, she sought a drug that would prevent their destruction even by mortal hands. But Zeus barred the appearance of Eos (the Dawn), Selene (the Moon), and Helios (the Sun), and chopped up the drug himself before Ge could find it."

According to The Living Torah, cannabis was an ingredient of holy anointing oil mentioned in various sacred Hebrew texts. The herb of interest is most commonly known as kaneh-bosm. This is mentioned several times in the Old Testament as a bartering material, incense, and an ingredient in holy anointing oil used by the high priest of the temple. Although most research in this area focuses on cannabis, there is mention of evidence suggesting use of additional visionary plants such as henbane, as well.

The Septuagint translates kaneh-bosm as calamus, and this translation has been propagated unchanged to most later translations of the old testament. However, Polish anthropologist Sula Benet published etymological arguments that the Aramaic word for hemp can be read as kannabos and appears to be a cognate to the modern word 'cannabis', with the root kan meaning reed or hemp and bosm meaning fragrant. Both cannabis and calamus are fragrant, reedlike plants containing psychotropic compounds.

Although philologist John Marco Allegro has suggested that the self-revelation and healing abilities attributed to the figure of Jesus may have been associated with the effects of the plant medicines. This evidence is dependent on pre-Septuagint interpretation of Torah and Tenach, and goes firmly against the accepted teachings of the Holy See. However Merkur contends that a minority of Christian hermits and mystics could possibly have used entheogens, in conjunction with fasting, meditation and prayer.

John Marco Allegro was the only non-Catholic appointed to the position of translating the Dead Sea scrolls. His extrapolations are often the object of scorn due to Allegro's non-mainstream theory of Jesus as a mythological personification of the essence of a "psychoactive sacrament", furthermore they conflict with the position of the Catholic Church in regards to transubstantiation and the teaching involving valid matter, form, and substance-that of bread and wine, which do not contain psychoactive substances.

Allegro's book, The Sacred Mushroom and the Cross, relates the development of language to the development of myths, religions and cultic practices in world cultures. Allegro believed he could prove, through etymology, that the roots of Christianity, as of many other religions, lay in fertility cults; and that cult practices, such as ingesting visionary plants, or "psychedelics", to perceive the Mind of God, persisted into the early Christian era, and to some unspecified extent into the 1200s with reoccurrences in the 1700s and mid 1900s, as he interprets the Plaincourault chapel's fresco to be an accurate depiction of the ritual ingestion of Amanita muscaria as the Eucharist.

The historical picture portrayed by the Entheos journal is of fairly widespread use of visionary plants in early Christianity and the surrounding culture, with a gradual reduction of use of entheogens in Christianity. R. Gordon Wasson's book Soma prints a letter from art historian Erwin Panofsky asserting that art scholars are aware of many 'mushroom trees' in Christian art.

The question of the extent of visionary plant use throughout the history of Christian practice has barely been considered yet by academic or independent scholars. The question of whether visionary plants were used in pre-Theodosius Christianity is distinct from evidence that indicates the extent to which visionary plants were utilized or forgotten in later Christianity, including so-called "heretical" or "quasi-" Christian groups, and the question of other groups such as elites or laity within "orthodox" Catholic practice.

Entheogens have played a pivotal role in the spiritual practices of most American cultures for millennia. The first American entheogen to be subject to scientific analysis was the peyote cactus. For his part, one of the founders of modern ethno-botany, the late Richard Evans Schultes of Harvard University documented the ritual use of peyote cactus among the Kiowa who live in what became Oklahoma.

Used traditionally by many cultures of what is now Mexico, its use spread to throughout North America in the 19th century, replacing the toxic entheogen Sophora secundiflora. Other well-known entheogens used by Mexican cultures include psilocybin mushrooms, known to indigenous Mexicans under the Náhuatl name teonanácatl, the seeds of several morning glories and Salvia divinorum.

In addition to indigenous use of entheogens in the Americas, one should also note their important role in contemporary religious movements, such as the Rastafari movement and the Church of the Universe.

Pharmaceutical Drugs

A pharmaceutical drug, also referred to as medicine, medication or medicament, can be loosely defined as any chemical substance intended for use in the medical diagnosis, cure, treatment, or prevention of disease.

Medications can be classified in various ways, such as by chemical properties, mode or route of administration, biological system affected, or therapeutic effects. An elaborate and widely used classification system is the Anatomical Therapeutic Chemical Classification System (ATC system). The World Health Organization keeps a list of essential medicines.

Medications may be divided into over-the-counter drugs (OTC) which may be available without special restrictions, and prescription only medicine (POM), which must be prescribed by a licensed medical practitioner. The precise distinction between OTC and prescription depends on the legal jurisdiction. A third category, behind-the-counter medications (BTMs), is implemented in some jurisdictions. BTMs do not require a prescription, but must be kept in the dispensary, not visible to the public, and only be sold by a pharmacist or pharmacy technician.

The International Narcotics Control Board of the United Nations imposes a world law of prohibition of certain medications. They publish a lengthy list of chemicals and plants whose trade and consumption is forbidden. OTC medications are sold without restriction as they are considered safe enough that most people will not hurt themselves accidentally by taking it as instructed. Many countries, such as the United Kingdom have a third category of pharmacy medicines which can only be sold in registered pharmacies, by or under the supervision of a pharmacist.

For patented medications, countries may have certain mandatory licensing programs which compel, in certain situations, a medication's owner to contract with other agents to manufacture the drug. Such programs may deal with the contingency of a lack of medication in the event of a serious epidemic of disease, or may be part of efforts to ensure that disease treating drugs, such as AIDS drugs, are available to countries which cannot afford the drug owner's price.

Since the 1990s water contamination by pharmaceuticals has been an environmental issue of concern. Most pharmaceuticals are deposited in the environment through human consumption and excretion, and are often filtered ineffectively by waste-water treatment plants which are not designed to manage them. Once in the water they can have diverse, subtle effects on organisms, although research is limited. Pharmaceuticals may also be deposited in the environment through improper disposal, runoff from sludge fertilizer and reclaimed waste-water irrigation, and leaky sewage.

In 2009 an investigative report by Associated Press concluded that U.S. manufacturers had legally released 271 million pounds of drugs into the environment, 92% of which was the antiseptics phenol and hydrogen peroxide. It could not distinguish between drugs released by manufacturers as opposed to the pharmaceutical industry. It also found that an estimated 250 million pounds of pharmaceuticals and contaminated packaging were discarded by hospitals and long-term care facilities.

* * *

Using plants and plant substances to treat all kinds of diseases and medical conditions is believed to date back to prehistoric medicine.

The Kahun Gynaecological Papyrus, the oldest known medical text of any kind, dates to about 1800 BC and represents the first documented use of any kind of medication. It and other medical papyri describe Ancient Egyptian medical practices, such as using honey to treat infections.

Ancient Babylonian medicine demonstrate the use of prescriptions in the first half of the 2nd millennium BC. Medicinal creams and pills were employed as treatments.

On the Indian subcontinent, the Atharvaveda, a sacred text of Hinduism whose core dates from sometime during the 2nd millennium BC, although the hymns recorded in it are believed to be older, is the first Indic text dealing with medicine. It describes plant-based medications to counter diseases. The earliest foundations of ayurveda were built on a synthesis of selected ancient herbal practices, together with a massive addition of theoretical conceptualizations, new nosologies and new therapies dating from about 400 BC onwards. The student of Āyurveda was expected to know ten arts that were indispensable in the preparation and application of his medicines: distillation, operative skills, cooking, horticulture, metallurgy, sugar manufacture, pharmacy, analysis and separation of minerals, compounding of metals, and preparation of alkalis.

The Hippocratic Oath for physicians, attributed to 5th century BC Greece, refers to the existence of "deadly drugs", and ancient Greek physicians imported medications from Egypt and elsewhere.

The first drugstores were created in Baghdad in the 8th century AD. The injection syringe was invented by Ammar ibn Ali al-Mawsili in 9th century Iraq. Al-Kindi's 9th century book, De Gradibus, developed a mathematical scale to quantify the strength of drugs.

The Canon of Medicine by Ibn Sina, who is considered the father of modern medicine, reported 800 tested drugs at the time of its completion in 1025 AD. The Canon is considered the first pharmacopoeia, or organized list of medications and their preparation. Ibn Sina's contributions include the separation of medicine from pharmacology, which was important to the development of the pharmaceutical sciences. Islamic medicine knew of at least 2,000 medicinal and chemical substances.

Medieval medicine saw advances in surgery, but few truly effective drugs existed, beyond opium and quinine. Folklore cures and potentially poisonous metal-based compounds were popular treatments. Theodoric Borgognoni, (1205-1296), one of the most significant surgeons of the medieval period, responsible for introducing and promoting important surgical advances including basic antiseptic practice and the use of anaesthetics. Garcia de Orta described some herbal treatments that were used.

For most of the nineteenth century, drugs were not highly effective, leading Oliver Wendell Holmes, Sr. to famously comment in 1842 that "if all medicines in the world were thrown into the sea, it would be all the better for mankind and all the worse for the fishes".

During the First World War, Alexis Carrel and Henry Dakin developed the Carrel-Dakin method of treating wounds with an irrigation, Dakin's solution, a germicide which helped prevent gangrene.

In the inter-war period, the first anti-bacterial agents such as the sulfa antibiotics were developed. The Second World War saw the introduction of widespread and effective antimicrobial therapy with the development and mass production of penicillin antibiotics, made possible by the pressures of the war and the collaboration of British scientists with the American pharmaceutical industry.

Medicines commonly used by the late 1920s included aspirin, codeine, and morphine for pain; digitalis, nitroglycerin, and quinine for heart disorders, and insulin for diabetes. Other drugs included antitoxins, a few biological vaccines, and a few synthetic drugs. In the 1930s antibiotics emerged: first sulfa drugs, then penicillin and other antibiotics. Drugs increasingly became "the center of medical practice". In the 1950s other drugs emerged including corticosteroids for inflammation, rauwolfia alkloids as tranqulizers and antihypertensives, antihistamines for nasal allergies, xanthines for asthma, and typical antipsychotics for psychosis. As of 2008, thousands of approved drugs have been developed. Increasingly, biotechnology is used to discover biopharmaceuticals.

In the 1950s new psychiatric drugs, notably the antipsychotic chlorpromazine, were designed in laboratories and slowly came into preferred use. Although often accepted as an advance in some ways, there was some opposition, due to serious adverse effects such as tardive dyskinesia. Patients often opposed psychiatry and refused or stopped taking the drugs when not subject to psychiatric control.

Governments have been heavily involved in the development and sale of drugs. In the U.S., the Elixir Sulfanilamide disaster led to the establishment of the Food and Drug Administration, and the 1938 Federal Food, Drug, and Cosmetic Act required manufacturers to file new drugs with the FDA. The 1951 Humphrey-Durham Amendment required certain drugs to be sold by prescription. In 1962 a subsequent amendment required new drugs to be tested for efficacy and safety in clinical trials.

Until the 1970s, drug prices were not a major concern for doctors and patients. As more drugs became prescribed for chronic illnesses, however, costs became burdensome, and by the 1970s nearly every U.S. state required or encouraged the substitution of generic drugs for higher-priced brand names. This also led to the 2006 U.S. law, Medicare Part D, which offers Medicare coverage for drugs.

As of 2008, the United States is the leader in medical research, including pharmaceutical development. U.S. drug prices are among the highest in the world, and drug innovation is correspondingly high. In 2000 U.S. based firms developed 29 of the 75 top-selling drugs; firms from the second-largest market, Japan, developed eight, and the United Kingdom contributed 10. France, which imposes price controls, developed three. Throughout the 1990s outcomes were similar.

Alcoholic Beverages

An alcoholic beverage is a drink that contains ethanol, commonly called alcohol. Alcoholic beverages are divided into three general classes: beers, wines, and spirits.

Alcoholic beverages are consumed in most sovereign states. Each nation has laws that regulate their production, sale, and consumption. In particular, such laws specify the minimum age at which a person may legally buy or drink them. The minimum age varies between 16 and 25 depending on the nation and the type of drink. Most nations set it at 18 years of age though the United States sets it at 21.

The production and consumption of alcohol occurs in most cultures of the world, from hunter-gatherer peoples to nation-states. Alcoholic beverages are often an important part of social events in these cultures. In many cultures, drinking plays a significant role in social interaction, mainly because of alcohol's neurological effects.

Alcohol is a psychoactive drug that has a depressant effect. A high blood alcohol content is usually considered to be legal drunkenness because it reduces attention and slows reaction speed. Alcoholic beverages can be addictive, and the state of addiction to alcohol is known as alcoholism.

Alcohol has been used by people around the world, in the standard diet, for hygienic/medical reasons, for its relaxant and euphoric effects, for recreational purposes, for artistic inspiration, as aphrodisiacs, and for other reasons. Some drinks have been invested with symbolic or religious significance suggesting the mystical use of alcohol, e.g. by Greco-Roman religion in the ecstatic rituals of Dionysus, also called Bacchus, the god of wine and revelry; in the Christian Eucharist; and on the Jewish Shabbat and festivals, particularly Passover.

Chemical analysis of traces absorbed and preserved in pottery jars from the Neolithic village of Jiahu, in Henan province, Northern China, have revealed that a mixed fermented beverage of rice, honey, and fruit was being produced as early as 9,000 years ago. This is approximately the same time that barley beer and grape wine were beginning to be made in the Middle East. Recipes have been found on clay tablets and art in Mesopotamia that show individuals using straws to drink beer from large vats and pots.

The Hindu Ayurvedic texts describe both the beneficent uses of alcoholic beverages and the consequences of intoxication and alcoholic diseases. Most of the peoples in India and China, have continued, throughout, to ferment a portion of their crops and nourish themselves with the alcoholic product. However, devout adherents of Buddhism, which arose in India in the 5th and 6th centuries BC and spread over southern and eastern Asia, abstain to this day, as do devout Hindus and Sikhs. In Mesopotamia and Egypt, the birthplace of beer and wine, Islam is now the predominant religion, and it also prohibits the drinking and even the handling of alcoholic beverages.

Wine was consumed in Classical Greece at breakfast or at symposia, and in the 1st century BC it was part of the diet of most Roman citizens. However, both Greeks and Romans generally consumed diluted wine (with strengths varying from 1 part wine and 1 part water to 1 part wine and 4 parts water).

The transformation of water into wine at the wedding at Cana is the first of the miracles attributed to Jesus in the New Testament, and His use of wine in the Last Supper led to it becoming an essential part of the Eucharist rite in most Christian traditions.

In Europe during the Middle Ages, beer was consumed by the whole family, thanks to a triple fermentation process-the men had the strongest, then women, then children. A document of the times mentions nuns having an allowance of six pints of ale a day. Cider and pomace wine were also widely available, while grape wine was the prerogative of the higher classes.

By the time the Europeans reached the Americas in the 15th century, several native civilizations had developed alcoholic beverages. According to a post-Conquest Aztec document, consumption of the local "wine" (pulque) was generally restricted to religious ceremonies, but freely allowed to those over 70 years old. The natives of South America manufactured a beer-like product from cassava or maize, which had to be chewed before fermentation in order to turn the starch into sugars. This chewing technique was also used in ancient Japan to make sake from rice and other starchy crops.

The medicinal use of alcohol was mentioned in Sumerian and Egyptian texts dated from 2100 BC or earlier. The Bible, in Proverbs 31:6-7, recommends giving alcoholic drinks to those who are dying or depressed, so that they can forget their misery.

The distillation of alcohol can be traced back to China, Central Asia and the Middle East. In particular, Muslim chemists were the first to produce fully purified distilled alcohol. It later spread to Europe in the mid-12th century, and by the early 14th century it had spread throughout the continent. It also spread eastward, mainly due to the Mongols, and began in China no later than the 14th century. Paracelsus gave alcohol its modern name, taking it from the Arabic word which means "finely divided", a reference to distillation.

In the early 19th century, Americans had inherited a hearty drinking tradition. Many different types of alcoholic beverages were consumed. One reason for this heavy drinking was an overabundance of corn on the western frontier. This overabundance encouraged the widespread production of cheap whiskey. It was at this time that alcoholic beverages became an important part of the American diet. In the mid 1820s, Americans drank seven gallons of alcohol per capita annually.

During the 19th century, Americans drank an abundance of alcohol and drank it in two distinctive ways. One way was to drink small amounts daily and regularly, usually at home or alone. The other way consisted of communal binges. Groups of people would gather in a public place for elections, court sessions, militia musters, holiday celebrations, or neighborly festivities. Participants would typically drink until they became intoxicated.

Alcoholic beverages that have a lower alcohol content (beer and wine) are produced by fermentation of sugar- or starch-containing plant material; beverages of higher alcohol content (spirits) are produced by fermentation followed by distillation.

Beer is the world's oldest and most widely consumed alcoholic beverage and the third most popular drink overall after water and tea. It is produced by the brewing and fermentation of starches which are mainly derived from cereal grains - most commonly malted barley although wheat, maize (corn), and rice are also used. Alcoholic beverages which are distilled after fermentation, fermented from non-cereal sources such as grapes or honey, or fermented from un-malted cereal grain, are not classified as beer.

Most beer is flavored with hops, which add bitterness and act as a natural preservative. Other flavorings, such as fruits or herbs, may also be used. The alcoholic strength of beer is usually 4% to 6% alcohol by volume (ABV), but it may be less than 1% or more than 20%.

Beer is part of the culture of various nations and has acquired social traditions such as beer festivals and pub culture, which involves activities such as pub crawling and pub games.

The basics of brewing beer are shared across national and cultural boundaries. The two main types of beer are lager and ale, which is further classified into varieties such as pale ale, stout, and brown ale. The beer-brewing industry is a global business, consisting of several dominant multinational companies and thousands of smaller producers, which range from brewpubs to regional breweries.

Wine involves a longer, and more complete, fermentation process and a long aging process, taking months or even years, that results in an alcohol content of 9%-16% ABV. Sparkling wine can be made by adding a small amount of sugar before bottling, which causes a secondary fermentation to occur in the bottle.

Unsweetened, distilled, alcoholic beverages that have an alcohol content of at least 20% ABV are called spirits. Spirits are produced by distillation of a fermented product; this process concentrates the alcohol and eliminates some of the congeners. Spirits can be added to wines to create fortified wines, such as port and sherry.

The names of some beverages are determined by the source of the material fermented. In general, a beverage fermented from a starch-heavy source such as a grain or potato, in which the starch must first be broken down into sugars by malting, will be called a beer. If the mash is distilled, the end product is a spirit. Wine is generally made from fermented grapes.

Brandy and wine are made only from grapes. If an alcoholic beverage is made from another kind of fruit, it is distinguished as fruit brandy or fruit wine. The variety of fruit must be specified, as "cherry brandy" or "plum wine".

In the USA and Canada, cider often means unfermented apple juice, while fermented cider is called hard cider. Unfermented cider is sometimes called sweet cider. In the UK, cider refers to the alcoholic drink; in Australia the term is ambiguous.

Beer is generally made from barley, but can sometimes contain a mix of other grains. Whiskey is sometimes made from a blend of different grains, especially Irish whiskey which may contain several different grains. The style of whiskey (Scotch, rye, Bourbon, corn) generally determines the primary grain used, with additional grains usually added to the blend. These additional grains are most often barley, and sometimes oats.

As far as American whiskey is concerned, Bourbon (corn), and rye whiskey, must be at least 51% of respective constituent at fermentation, while corn whiskey (as opposed to Bourbon) must be at least 81%-all by American law similar to the French A.O.C (Appellation d'Origine Controlée).

Two common distilled beverages are vodka and gin. Vodka can be distilled from any source of agricultural origin, grain and potatoes being the most common, but the main characteristic of vodka is that it is so thoroughly distilled as to exhibit less of the flavors derived from its source material. Some distillers and experts, however, may disagree, arguing that potato vodkas display a creamy mouth-feel, while rye vodkas will have heavy nuances of rye. Other vodkas may display citrus notes.

Gin is a similar distillate which has been flavored by contact with herbs and other plant products-especially juniper berries, but also including angel root, licorice, cardamom, grains of paradise, Bulgarian rose petals, and many others.

Applejack is an example of a drink originally made by freeze distillation, which is easy to do in cold climates. Although both distillation and freeze distillation reduce the water content, they are not equivalent, because freeze distillation concentrates poisonous higher alcohols rather than reducing them like distillation.

The concentration of alcohol in a beverage is usually stated as the percentage of alcohol by volume (ABV) or, in the United States, as proof. In the U.S.A., proof is twice the percentage of alcohol by volume at 60 degrees Fahrenheit (e.g., 80 proof = 40% ABV). Degrees proof were formerly used in the United Kingdom, where 100 degrees proof was equivalent to 57.1% ABV. Historically, this was the most dilute spirit that would sustain the combustion of gunpowder.

Ordinary distillation cannot produce alcohol of more than 95.6% ABV (191.2 proof) because at that point alcohol is an azeotrope with water. Alcohol of this high level of purity is commonly called neutral grain spirit.

Most yeasts cannot reproduce when the concentration of alcohol is higher than about 18%, so that is the practical limit for the strength of fermented beverages such as wine, beer, and sake. Strains of yeast have been developed that can reproduce in solutions of up to 25% ABV.

At times and places of poor public sanitation, such as Medieval Europe, the consumption of alcoholic drinks was a way of avoiding water-borne diseases such as cholera. Small beer and faux wine, in particular, were used for this purpose. Although alcohol kills bacteria, its low concentration in these beverages would have had only a limited effect. More important was that the boiling of water, which was required for the brewing of beer, and the growth of yeast, required for fermentation of beer and wine, would tend to kill dangerous microorganisms. The alcohol content of these beverages allowed them to be stored for months or years in simple wood or clay containers without spoiling. For this reason, they were commonly kept aboard sailing vessels as an important source of hydration for the crew, especially during the long voyages of the early modern period.

In cold climates, strong alcoholic beverages such as vodka are popularly seen as a way to "warm up" the body, possibly because alcohol is a quickly absorbed source of food energy and because it dilates peripheral blood vessels. This is a misconception because the perception of warmth is actually caused by the transfer of heat from the body's core to its extremities, where it is quickly lost to the environment.

Studies have found that when food is eaten before drinking alcohol, alcohol absorption is reduced and the rate at which alcohol is eliminated from the blood is increased. The mechanism for the faster alcohol elimination appears to be unrelated to the type of food. The likely mechanism is food-induced increases in alcohol-metabolizing enzymes and liver blood flow

Alcohol intoxication affects the brain, causing slurred speech, clumsiness, and delayed reflexes. Alcohol stimulates insulin production, which speeds up the glucose metabolism and can result in low blood sugar, causing irritability, and possibly death for diabetics; in normal subjects severe alcohol poisoning can also be lethal. A blood alcohol content of 0.45 represents the LD50, or the amount which would prove fatal in 50% of test subjects. This is about six times the level of intoxication (0.08%), but vomiting and/or unconsciousness are triggered much sooner in people with a low tolerance, among whom such high levels are rarely reached unless a large amount of alcohol is consumed very quickly. However, chronic heavy drinkers' high tolerance may allow some of them to remain conscious at levels above .4%, despite the serious health dangers.

A 2001 report estimated that medium and high consumption of alcohol led to 75,754 deaths in the USA. Low consumption has some beneficial effects, so a net 59,180 deaths were attributed to alcohol. In the U.K., heavy drinking is blamed for up to 33,000 deaths a year.

A study in Sweden found that 29% to 44% of "unnatural" deaths, or deaths not caused by illness, were related to alcohol. The causes of death included suicide, falls, traffic injuries, asphyxia, intoxication and murder.

A global study found that 3.6% of all cancer cases worldwide are caused by alcohol drinking, resulting in 3.5% of all global cancer deaths. A U.K. study found that alcohol causes about 6% of cancer deaths in the U.K., killing over 9,000 people a year.

Alcohol expectations are beliefs that individuals hold about the effects they experience from drinking. They are largely beliefs about how the consumption of alcohol will affect a person's emotions, abilities and behaviors. To the extent that alcohol expectancies can be changed, it may be possible to reduce a major social and health problem, that of alcohol abuse.

If people in a society generally believe that intoxication leads to aggression, sexual behavior AKA "beer goggles", or rowdy behavior, they tend to act that way when intoxicated. If the society teaches that intoxication leads to relaxation and tranquil behavior, it virtually always leads to those outcomes. Alcohol expectations vary within a population so outcomes are not uniform.

People tend to conform to social expectations and a common belief in most societies is that alcohol causes disinhibition. However, in those societies in which people don't believe that alcohol disinhibits, intoxication virtually never leads to unacceptable behaviors because of "disinhibition".

Alcohol expectations can operate in the absence of actual consumption of alcohol. Research in the U.S. over a period of decades has shown that men tend to become physically more sexually aroused when they think they have been drinking alcohol, even when they haven't. Women report feeling more sexually aroused when they falsely believe the beverages they have been consuming contain alcohol, although a measure of their physiological arousal shows that they are physically becoming less aroused.

Men tend to become more aggressive in laboratory studies in which they are drinking only tonic water but believe that it contains alcohol. They also become relatively less aggressive when they think they are drinking only tonic water, but are actually drinking tonic containing alcohol.

The phenomenon of alcohol expectations recognizes that intoxication has real physiological consequences affecting perceptions of space and time, reducing psychomotor skills, disrupting equilibrium and a number of other behaviors.

The manner and degree to which alcohol expectations interact with the physiological effects of intoxication to yield the behavior that results is unclear.

Some religions-most notably Islam, Sikhism, Jainism, the Bahá'í Faith, The Church of Jesus Christ of Latter-day Saints, the Seventh-day Adventist Church, the Church of Christ, Scientist, the United Pentecostal Church International, Theravada, most Mahayana schools of Buddhism, some Protestant sects of Fundamentalist Christianity, and some sects of Hinduism-forbid, discourage, or restrict the drinking of alcoholic beverages for various reasons.

Many Christian denominations use wine in the Eucharist or Communion and permit the use of alcohol in moderation, while others use unfermented grape juice in Communion and abstain from alcohol by choice or prohibit it outright.

Judaism uses wine on Shabbat for Kiddush as well as in the Passover ceremony and in other religious ceremonies, including Purim, and allows the use of alcohol, such as kosher wine. Many ancient Jewish texts such as the Talmud even encourage moderate amounts of drinking on holidays such as Purim, in order to make the occasion more joyous.

Buddhist texts recommend refraining from drugs and alcohol, because they may inhibit mindfulness.

Some pagan religions, however, had a completely opposite view of alcohol and drunkenness; they actively promoted them as means of fostering fertility. Alcohol was thought to increase sexual desire and to lower the threshold of approaching another person for sex. For example, Norse paganism considered alcohol to be the sap of Yggdrasil, and drunkenness was an important fertility rite in this religion. Paradoxically, one of the effects of alcohol intoxication is the reduction of sexual arousal.

Some countries forbid the production and consumption of alcoholic beverages.

In the United States, there was an attempt from 1920 to 1933 to eliminate the consumption of alcoholic beverages through national prohibition of their manufacture and sale. This period became known as the prohibition era. During this period the 18th Amendment to the Constitution of the United States made manufacture, sale and transportation of alcoholic beverages illegal throughout the United States. However, this project led to the unintended consequences of causing widespread disrespect for the law as many people sought alcoholic beverages from illegal sources, and of creating a lucrative business for illegal purveyors of alcohol, or bootleggers, which led to the development of organized crime. As a result prohibition became widely unpopular, leading to repeal of the 18th Amendment in 1933. Prior to national prohibition, beginning in the late 19th century, many states and localities had enacted prohibition within their jurisdictions, and following repeal of the 18th Amendment, some communities in the United States, now known as dry counties, still ban alcohol sales.

The Nordic countries, Norway and Finland, also had a period of alcohol prohibition in the early 20th century. This was the result of social democratic campaigning. Prohibition did not have popular support resulting in large-scale smuggling. Following the end of prohibition, state alcohol monopolies were established with detailed restrictions and high taxes. Some restrictions have been lifted. For example, supermarkets in Finland are allowed to sell only fermented beverages with an alcohol content up to 4.7%, but Alko, the government monopoly, is allowed to sell wine and spirits. This is also the case with the Swedish Systembolaget and the Norwegian Vinmonopolet.

In Iceland, beer with an alcohol percentage of 2.25% or less is sold in supermarkets. Stronger beer, wine or other spirits are sold in 'Vinbudin'.

Some Muslim countries, such as Saudi Arabia, prohibit alcohol for religious reasons.

The legal age for purchase or possession, but not necessarily consumption, in every state has been 21 since shortly after the passage of the National Minimum Drinking Age Act in 1984, which tied federal highway funds to states' maintaining a minimum drinking age of 21.

Eighteen states (Arkansas, California, Connecticut, Florida, Georgia, Kentucky, Maryland, Massachusetts, Mississippi, Missouri, Nevada, New Hampshire, New Mexico, New York, Oklahoma, Rhode Island, South Carolina, and Wyoming) and the District of Columbia have laws against possession of alcohol by minors but do not prohibit its consumption by minors.

Thirteen states (Alaska, Colorado, Delaware, Illinois, Louisiana, Maine, Minnesota, Missouri, Montana, Ohio, Oregon, Texas, and Wisconsin) specifically permit minors to drink alcohol given to them by their parents or a by a person whom their parents see fit.

Many states also specifically permit consumption under the age of 21 for religious or health reasons.

In the United States, the sale of alcoholic beverages is controlled by the individual states, the counties or parishes within each state, and then by local jurisdictions within counties. For example, in most of North Carolina, beer and wine may be purchased in retail stores, but distilled spirits are only available at state ABC (Alcohol Beverage Control) stores. In Maryland, distilled spirits are available in liquor stores except in Montgomery County where the county runs the ABC stores. A county that prohibits the sale of alcohol is known as a dry county.

In most states, individuals may freely produce wine and beer usually up to 100 gallons per adult per year, but no more than 200 gallons per household per year for personal consumption, but not for sale. However, in St. Mary's County, Maryland, a "bona fide" resident may sell beer and native wines from their home.

The production of distilled beverages is regulated and taxed. The Bureau of Alcohol, Tobacco, Firearms, and Explosives and the Alcohol and Tobacco Tax and Trade Bureau (formerly one organization known as the Bureau of Alcohol, Tobacco and Firearms) enforce federal laws and regulations related to alcohol. Illegal manufacture of distilled liquor is often referred to as "moon shining," and the product, which is not aged and contains a high percentage of alcohol, is often called "white lightning."

All alcoholic product packaging sold in the United States must contain a health warning from the Surgeon General.

In the United Kingdom, the Customs and Excise department issues distilling licenses. New Zealand is one of the few countries where it is not only legal to produce any form of alcohol for personal use, including spirits, it is neither taxed nor licensed. This has made the sale and use of home distillation equipment popular.

Tobacco

Tobacco is an agricultural product processed from the leaves of plants in the genus Nicotiana. It can be consumed, used as an organic pesticide, and, in the form of nicotine tartrate, it is used in some medicines. In consumption it most commonly appears in the forms of smoking, chewing, snuffing, or dipping tobacco, or snus. Tobacco has long been in use as an entheogen in the Americas. However, upon the arrival of Europeans in North America, it quickly became popularized as a trade item and as a recreational drug.

This popularization led to the development of the southern economy of the United States until it gave way to cotton. Following the American Civil War, a change in demand and a change in labor force allowed for the development of the cigarette. This new product quickly led to the growth of tobacco companies, until the scientific controversy of the mid-1900s.

There are many species of tobacco, which are all encompassed by the plant genus Nicotiana. The word nicotiana (as well as nicotine) was named in honor of Jean Nicot, French ambassador to Portugal, who in 1559 sent it as a medicine to the court of Catherine de Medici.

Because of the addictive properties of nicotine, tolerance and dependence develop. Absorption quantity, frequency, and speed of tobacco consumption are believed to be directly related to biological strength of nicotine dependence, addiction, and tolerance. The usage of tobacco is an activity that is practiced by some 1.1 billion people, and up to 1/3 of the adult population. The World Health Organization reports it to be the leading preventable cause of death worldwide and estimates that it currently causes 5.4 million deaths per year. Rates of smoking have leveled off or declined in developed countries, however they continue to rise in developing countries.

Tobacco is cultivated similarly to other agricultural products. Seeds are sown in cold frames or hotbeds to prevent attacks from insects, and then transplanted into the fields. Tobacco is an annual crop, which is usually harvested mechanically or by hand. After harvest, tobacco is stored for curing, which allows for the slow oxidation and degradation of carotenoids. This allows for the agricultural product to take on properties that are usually attributed to the "smoothness" of the smoke. Following this, tobacco is packed into its various forms of consumption, which include smoking, chewing, sniffing, and so on.

Tobacco had already long been used in the Americas when European settlers arrived and introduced the practice to Europe, where it became popular. At high doses, tobacco can become hallucinogenic. Native Americans never used the drug for recreational purposes. Instead, it was often consumed as an entheogen. Among some tribes, this was done only by experienced shamans or medicine men. Eastern North American tribes would carry large amounts of tobacco in pouches as a readily accepted trade item, and would often smoke it in pipes, either in defined ceremonies that were considered sacred, or to seal a bargain, and they would smoke it at such occasions in all stages of life, even in childhood. It is believed that tobacco is a gift from the Creator and that the exhaled tobacco smoke carries one's thoughts and prayers to heaven.

Following the arrival of the Europeans, tobacco became increasingly popular as a trade item. It fostered the economy for the southern United States until it was replaced by cotton. Following the American civil war, a change in demand and a change in labor force allowed inventor James Bonsack to create a machine which automated cigarette production.

This increase in production allowed tremendous growth in the tobacco industry until the scientific revelations of the mid-1900s.

Following the scientific revelations of the mid-1900s, tobacco became condemned as a health hazard, and eventually became encompassed as a cause for cancer, as well as other respiratory and circulatory diseases. This led to the Tobacco Master Settlement Agreement (MSA) which settled the lawsuit in exchange for a combination of yearly payments to the states and voluntary restrictions on advertising and marketing of tobacco products.

In the 1970s, Brown & Williamson cross-bred a strain of tobacco to produce Y1. This strain of tobacco contained an unusually high amount of nicotine, nearly doubling its content from 3.2-3.5% to 6.5%. In the 1990s, this prompted the Food and Drug Administration (FDA) to use this strain as evidence that tobacco companies were intentionally manipulating the nicotine content of cigarettes.

In 2003, in response to growth of tobacco use in developing countries, the World Health Organization successfully rallied 168 countries to sign the Framework Convention on Tobacco Control. The Convention is designed to push for effective legislation and its enforcement in all countries to reduce the harmful effects of tobacco. This led to the development of tobacco cessation products.

Smoking in public was for a long time something reserved for men, and when done by women was sometimes associated with promiscuity. In Japan during the Edo period, prostitutes and their clients would often approach one another under the guise of offering a smoke, and the same was true for 19th century Europe.

Following the American Civil War the usage of tobacco, primarily in cigarettes, became associated with masculinity and power, and is an iconic image associated with the stereotypical capitalist. Today, tobacco is often rejected; this has spawned quitting associations and anti-smoking campaigns. Bhutan is the only country in the world where tobacco sales are illegal.

Research is limited mainly to tobacco smoking, which has been studied the more extensively than any other form of consumption. As of 2000, smoking is practiced by some 1.22 billion people, of which men are more likely to smoke than women, however, the gender gap declines with age. Poor more likely than rich, and people in developing countries or transitional economies are more likely than people in developed countries. As of 2004, the World Health Organization reports that of the 58.8 million deaths to occur globally, 5.4 million are tobacco-attributed.

Tobacco use leads most commonly to diseases affecting the heart and lungs, with smoking being a major risk factor for heart attacks, strokes, chronic obstructive pulmonary disease (COPD), emphysema, and cancer.

The World Health Organization estimates that tobacco caused 5.4 million deaths in 2004 and 100 million deaths over the course of the 20th century. Similarly, the United States Centers for Disease Control and Prevention describes tobacco use as "the single most important preventable risk to human health in developed countries and an important cause of premature death worldwide."

Rates of smoking have leveled off or declined in the developed world. Smoking rates in the United States have dropped by half from 1965 to 2006, falling from 42% to 20.8% in adults. In the developing world, tobacco consumption is rising by 3.4% per year.

When the market for tobacco reduced in the West, the industry looked to India and China for 'emerging markets'. Dr. Sharad Vaidya, a cancer surgeon worked tirelessly to fight this, through research, advocacy and passion. He successfully raised awareness, introduced it in the curriculum of children and managed to establish legislation banning public smoking, stopping sports sponsorship, and sale to minors.

"Much of the disease burden and premature mortality attributable to tobacco use disproportionately affect the poor", and of the 1.22 billion smokers, 1 billion of them live in developing or transitional economies.

In Indonesia, the lowest income group spends 15% of its total expenditures on tobacco. In Egypt, more than 10% of households expediture in low-income homes is on tobacco. The poorest 20% of households in Mexico spend 11% of their income on tobacco.

The tobacco lobby gives money to politicians to vote in favor of deregulating tobacco. It is estimated that the United States tobacco lobby spends an average of $106,415 each day legislature meets; however the industry lost its support when the U.S. National Association of Attorneys General (NAAG) filed charges against the Tobacco Institute, a tobacco industry advocacy group. This resulted in the Master Settlement Agreement, which forced the organization to disband and place all records on a website.

Tobacco is cultivated similar to other agricultural products. Seeds were at first quickly scattered onto the soil. However, young plants came under increasing attack from flea beetles, which caused destruction of half the tobacco crops in United States in 1876. By 1890 successful experiments were conducted that placed the plant in a frame covered by thin fabric. Today, tobacco is sown in cold frames or hotbeds, as their germination is activated by light.

In the United States, tobacco is often fertilized with the mineral apatite, which partially starves the plant of nitrogen, to produce a more desired flavor. Apatite, however, contains radium, lead 210, and polonium 210, which are known radioactive carcinogens.

After the plants have reached relative maturity, they are transplanted into the fields, in which a relatively large hole is created in the tilled earth with a tobacco peg. Various mechanical tobacco planters were invented in the nineteenth and twentieth centuries to automate the process: making the hole, fertilizing it, guiding the plant in, all in one motion.

Tobacco is cultivated annually, and can be harvested in several ways. In the oldest method, the entire plant is harvested at once by cutting off the stalk at the ground with a sickle. In the nineteenth century, bright tobacco began to be harvested by pulling individual leaves off the stalk as they ripened. The leaves ripen from the ground upwards, so a field of tobacco may go through several so-called "pullings," more commonly known as topping (topping always refers to the removal of the tobacco flower before the leaves are systematically removed and, eventually, entirely harvested. As the industrial revolution took hold, harvesting wagons used to transport leaves were equipped with man-powered stringers, an apparatus which used twine to attach leaves to a pole. In modern times, large fields are harvested mechanically or by hand, although topping the flower and in some cases the plucking of immature leaves is still done by hand.

The Everybody Profits Method

Now I will introduce to you my proven method for living large, and free, as a "dealer in all things dope". If you follow the next few steps, just as they are written, I will personally guarantee that you will profit more, and faster, than any other dealer in your area. Not only will you profit, but the entire community will profit too. So, this means that you will hit the big time with this, but everybody wins. Isn't that the greatest thing in the world?

* * *

The first step in this method is for you, the dealer extraordinaire, to contact your supplier and tell him you need large quantities (for those who don't understand big words, that means a lot of product) and that you need it quick. If he asks questions, tell him that you have a big time buyer "downtown".

It is very important that you do not answer too many questions. Avoid saying anything about your "client" to your supplier, just generalize.

* * *

Next, go to the doughnut shop and pick up a couple of boxes of doughnuts. This "suggestive" gesture will help your sale go much smoother and may get you repeat business. It is important to remember not to discriminate against the doughnuts. Get a mixture of all types.

* * *

Hop on your bike, jump in your whip, hop in your hooptie or whatever you use to get around. Drive downtown to the building with all those cars with red and blue lights on them and walk inside the building. The building may be called the Police Department.

Don't let the name fool you though. This sale will be your best yet. If it isn't everything I promise, and you can prove you followed all these steps, I will refund your money for this book...maybe.

* * *

Walk up to the person behind the desk and say the following:

"Hello, my name is (insert name here) *and I have brought your office some free doughnuts. I would also like to know if anyone would like to purchase some of my fine products. Today I am selling drugs at a discount price. I have with me today the following products* (name all your products). *"*

The person behind the desk may ask you to wait a minute. If they do, ask if you can have a seat. Don't be surprised if you receive a lot of attention. This is commonplace for a new dealer with these folks.

When the proper person or people come to purchase your products, don't get scared and run, just repeat the lines above. It also helps if you have the products out. Just remember, don't try it before they buy it.

* * *

Now they will probably make you do some paperwork and have your picture taken so that they know their new sales representative. This is all standard procedure and is expected.

This entire process may take several hours, but you will be introduced to several other potential clients. You are well on your way to making it big time.

* * *

Now it is time to reap the rewards of your hard work. By now, you have an awesome free apartment, free food, free utilities and free clothes. It is probably safe to say that you will be their guest for the next several years and that you will be well taken care of. When the time comes for them to release you from your contract, you may wish to repeat the steps again and live for free for a few more years.

I hope that this method works for you and that you have all the luck in the world. Just keep in mind when you are living in your free apartment, don't drop the soap.

Sources and References

- "Dorlands Medical Dictionary".

- Lanni C, Lenzken SC, Pascale A, et al. (March 2008). "Cognition enhancers between treating and doping the mind". Pharmacol. Res. 57 (3): 196-213.

- Sahakian B, Morein-Zamir S (December 2007). "Professor's little helper". Nature 450 (7173): 1157-9.

- ""Towards responsible use of cognitive-enhancing drugs by the healthy" in Nature: International Weekly Journal of Science".

- "Smart Drugs and Should We Take Them?". Dolan DNA Learning Center.

- Malik R, Sangwan A, Saihgal R, Jindal DP, Piplani P (2007). "Towards better brain management: nootropics". Curr. Med. Chem. 14 (2): 123-31.

- Goldman P (2001). "Herbal medicines today and the roots of modern pharmacology". Ann. Intern. Med. 135 (8 Pt 1): 594-600.

- Bliss, Rosalie M. (2007). Agricultural Research 55 (10): 14-16.

- Chillot, R. (2004). Prevention 56 (1): 122-165.

- Gómez-Pinilla, F. (2008). "Brain foods: the effects of nutrients on brain function". Nature Reviews Neuroscience 9 (7): 568-578.

- Blaun, R., & Wiesenack, A. (1996). Psychology Today 29 (3): 34-35.

- Rogers, P. (2007). "Caffeine, mood and mental performance in everyday life.". Psychology Today 32 (1): 84-89.

- Kiefer, I. (2007). Scientific American Mind 18 (5): 58-63.

- Shukitt-Hale, B., Cheng, V., & Joseph, J. (2009). "Effects of blackberries on motor and cognitive function in aged rats". Nutritional Neuroscience 12 (3): 135-140.

- Wong, M., Emery, P., Preedy, V., & Wiseman, H. (2008). "Health benefits of isoflavones in functional foods? Proteomic and metabonomic advances.". Inflammopharmacology 16 (5): 235-239.

- Jia, X., McNeill, G., & Avenell, A. (2008). "Does taking vitamin, mineral and fatty acid supplements prevent cognitive decline? A systematic review of randomized controlled trials.". Journal of Human Nutrition & Dietetics 21 (4): 317-336.

- McDaniel, M.A., Maier, S.F., and Einstein, G.O. (2002). "Brain-Specific Nutrients: A Memory Cure?". Psychological Science in the Public Interest (American Psychological Society)' 3 (1): 957.

- Gualtieri F, Manetti D, Romanelli MN, Ghelardini C (2002). "Design and study of piracetam-like nootropics, controversial members of the problematic class of cognition-enhancing drugs". Curr. Pharm. Des. 8 (2): 125-38.

- "Popping Smart Pills: The Case for Cognitive Enhancement - TIME".

- Soman I, Mengi SA, Kasture SB (September 2004). "Effect of leaves of Butea frondosa on stress, anxiety, and cognition in rats". Pharmacol. Biochem. Behav. 79 (1): 11-6.

- Template:Anonymous. (2007). Boosting Our Knowledge of Brain Food. Agricultural Research, 55(10),14-16.

- Singh, H.K. and Dhawan, B.N. (1 September 1997). "Neuropsychopharmacological effects of the Ayurvedic nootropic Bacopa monniera Linn. (Brahmi)". Indian Journal of Pharmacology 29 (5): 359-65.

- Joshi H, Parle M (March 2006). "Brahmi rasayana improves learning and memory in mice". Evid Based Complement Alternat Med 3 (1): 79-85.

- Britton A, Singh-Manoux A, Marmot M (August 2004). "Alcohol consumption and cognitive function in the Whitehall II Study". Am. J. Epidemiol. 160 (3): 240-7.

- Launer LJ, Feskens EJ, Kalmijn S, Kromhout D (February 1996). "Smoking, drinking, and thinking. The Zutphen Elderly Study". Am. J. Epidemiol. 143 (3): 219-27.

- Galanis DJ, Joseph C, Masaki KH, Petrovitch H, Ross GW, White L (August 2000). "A longitudinal study of drinking and cognitive performance in elderly Japanese American men: the Honolulu-Asia Aging Study". Am J Public Health 90 (8): 1254-9.

- Dufouil C, Ducimetière P, Alpérovitch A (September 1997). "Sex differences in the association between alcohol consumption and cognitive performance. EVA Study Group. Epidemiology of Vascular Aging". Am. J. Epidemiol. 146 (5): 405-12.

- Rodgers B, Windsor TD, Anstey KJ, Dear KB, F Jorm A, Christensen H (September 2005). "Non-linear relationships between cognitive function and alcohol consumption in young, middle-aged and older adults: the PATH Through Life Project". Addiction 100 (9): 1280-90.

- Anstey KJ, Windsor TD, Rodgers B, Jorm AF, Christensen H (September 2005). "Lower cognitive test scores observed in alcohol abstainers are associated with demographic, personality, and biological factors: the PATH Through Life Project". Addiction 100 (9): 1291-301.

- "Brazilian Archives of Biology and Technology - Jurema-Preta

- Griffiths; Richards; McCann; Jesse (2006), "Psilocybin can occasion mystical-type experiences having substantial and sustained personal meaning and spiritual significance", Journal of Psychopharmacology 187: 268,

- Giorgio Samorini, "The 'Mushroom-Tree' of Plaincourault", Eleusis: Journal of Psychoactive Plants and Compounds, n. 8, 1997, pp. 29-37

- Giorgio Samorini, "The 'Mushroom-Trees' in Christian Art", Eleusis: Journal of Psychoactive Plants and Compounds, n. 1, 1998, pp. 87-108

- Heinrich, C (1995). Strange Fruit: Alchemy and Religion- The Hidden Truth. London : Bloomsbury. Referenced throughout ISBN 978-0747515487

- Kaplan, Aryeh. (1981). The Living Torah New York. p. 442.

- Sex, Drugs, Violence and the Bible, by Chris Bennett and Neil McQueen, 2001, Forbidden Fruit Publishing.

- Conjuring Eden: Art and the Entheogenic Vision of Paradise, by Mark Hoffman, Carl Ruck, and Blaise Staples. Entheos: The Journal of Psychedelic Spirituality, Issue No. 1, Summer, 2001

- Wasson and Allegro on the Tree of Knowledge as Amanita, Michael S. Hoffman, Journal of Higher Criticism, 2007

- Daturas for the Virgin, José Celdrán and Carl Ruck, Entheos: The Journal of Psychedelic Spirituality, Vol. I, Issue 2, Winter, 2002

- The Hidden World: Survival of Pagan Shamanic Themes in European Fairytales, by Carl Ruck, Blaise Staples, Jose Alfredo Celdran, Mark Hoffman, Carolina Academic Press, 2007

- Amanita Muscaria Mushrooms and Religion - Research Page

- Tupper, K.W. (2003). Entheogens & education: Exploring the potential of psychoactives as educational tools. Journal of Drug Education and Awareness, 1(2), 145-161.

- Tupper, K.W. (2002). Entheogens and existential intelligence: The use of plant teachers as cognitive tools. Canadian Journal of Education, 27(4), 499-516.

- Bwiti: An Ethnography of the Religious Imagination in Africa by James W. Fernandez, Princeton University Press, 1982

- Allegro, John Marco (1970). The Sacred Mushroom and the Cross: A Study of the Nature and Origins of Christianity within the Fertility Cults of the Ancient Near East. Hodder and Stoughton. ISBN 0-340-12875-5.

- US Federal Food, Drug, and Cosmetic Act, SEC. 210., (g)(1)(B).

- Directive 2004/27/EC of the European Parliament and of the Council of 31 March 2004 amending Directive 2001/83/EC on the Community code relating to medicinal products for human use. Article 1. Published March 31, 2004.

- Pharmaceutical Market Trends, 2006-2010, from Urch Publishing

- Blockbuster Drugs 2006: Executive Overview, from Report Buyer

- Doerr-MacEwen NA, Haight ME (November 2006). "Expert stakeholders' views on the management of human pharmaceuticals in the environment". Environ Manage 38 (5): 853-66.

- Donn J. (2009). Tons of Released Drugs Taint U.S. Water. AP.

- Griffith, F. Ll. The Petrie Papyri: Hieratic Papyri from Kahun and Gurob

- The Kahun Gynaecological Papyrus

- H. F. J. Horstmanshoff, Marten Stol, Cornelis Tilburg (2004), Magic and Rationality in Ancient Near Eastern and Graeco-Roman Medicine, p. 99, Brill Publishers, ISBN 9004136665.

- Kenneth G. Zysk, Asceticism and Healing in Ancient India: Medicine in the Buddhist Monastery, Oxford University Press, rev. ed. (1998) ISBN 0195059565

- Heinrich Von Staden, Herophilus: The Art of Medicine in Early Alexandria (Cambridge: Cambridge University Press, 1989), pp. 1-26.

- Felix Klein-Frank (2001), Al-Kindi, in Oliver Leaman and Hossein Nasr, History of Islamic Philosophy, p. 172. Routledge, London.

- Cas Lek Cesk (1980). "The father of medicine, Avicenna, in our science and culture: Abu Ali ibn Sina (980-1037)", Becka J. 119 (1), p. 17-23.

- Hitti, Philip K. (cf. Ajram, Kasem (1992), Miracle of Islamic Science, Appendix B, Knowledge House Publishers. ISBN 0911119434).

- Idrisi, Z. (2005). The Muslim Agricultural Revolution and its influence on Europe. The Foundation for Science, Technology and Civilization, UK.

- Bashar Saad, Hassan Azaizeh, Omar Said (October 2005). "Tradition and Perspectives of Arab Herbal Medicine: A Review", Evidence-based Complementary and Alternative Medicine 2 (4), p. 475-479 [476]. Oxford University Press.

- S. Hadzovic (1997). "Pharmacy and the great contribution of Arab-Islamic science to its development", Med Arh. 51 (1-2), p. 47-50.

- Finkelstein S, Temin P (2008). Reasonable Rx: Solving the drug price crisis. FT Press.

- Arnold, John P (2005). Origin and History of Beer and Brewing: From Prehistoric Times to the Beginning of Brewing Science and Technology. Cleveland, Ohio: Reprint Edition by BeerBooks. ISBN 0-9662084-1-2.

- Nelson, Max. "The Barbarian's Beverage: A History of Beer in Ancient Europe".

- Lichine, Alexis. Alexis Lichine's New Encyclopedia of Wines & Spirits (5th edition) (New York: Alfred A. Knopf, 1987), 707-709.

- Nutt D, King LA, Saulsbury W, Blakemore C (March 2007). "Development of a rational scale to assess the harm of drugs of potential misuse". Lancet 369 (9566): 1047-53.

- Ramchandani VA, Kwo PY, Li TK (December 2001). "Effect of food and food composition on alcohol elimination rates in healthy men and women". J Clin Pharmacol 41 (12): 1345-50.

- Meyer, Jerold S. and Linda F. Quenzer. Psychopharmacology: Drugs, the Brain, and Behavior. Sinauer Associates, Inc: Sunderland, Massachusetts. 2005. Page 228.

- "Alcohol-Attributable Deaths and Years of Potential Life Lost --- United States, 2001". Centers for Disease Control and Prevention. 2004-09-24.

- "Burden of alcohol-related cancer substantial". Abramson Cancer Center of the University of Pennsylvania. 2006-08-03.

- "Moderate Drinking Lowers Women's Risk Of Heart Attack". Science Daily. 2007-05-25.

- A L Klatsky and G D Friedman (1995-01). "Alcohol and longevity". American Journal of Public Health (American Public Health Association) 85 (1): 16-8.

- H Rodgers, PD Aitken, JM French, RH Curless, D Bates and OF James (1993). "Alcohol and stroke. A case-control study of drinking habits past and present". Stroke (AHA Journals) 24: 1473-1477.

- Richard Doll*, Richard Peto, Jillian Boreham and Isabelle Sutherland (2005). "Mortality in relation to alcohol consumption: a prospective study among male British doctors". International Journal of Epidemiology (Oxford Journals) 34 (1): 199-204.

- Grattan, K.E. and Vogel-Sprott. Maintaining intentional control of behavior under alcohol. Alcoholism, clinical and experimental research. 2001 Feb;25(2):192-197.

- Marlatt, G. A. and Rosenow. "The think-drink effect". Psychology Today, 1981, 15, 60-93.

- MacAndrew, C. and Edgerton. Drunken Comportment: A Social Explanation. Chicago: Aldine, 1969.

- Calgary Herald. "Last call for happy hour". Calgary Herald, August 1, 2008. Retrieved 15 July 2009.

- George F. Will (2009-10-29). "A reality check on drug use". Washington Post. Washington Post. pp. A19.

- Rorabaugh, W.J. (1981). The Alcoholic Republic: An American Tradition. Oxford University Press, USA. ISBN 9780195029901.

- Galanter, Marc; Kleber, Herbert D. (1 July 2008). The American Psychiatric Publishing Textbook of Substance Abuse Treatment (4th ed.). United States of America: American Psychiatric Publishing Inc. p. 114. ISBN 978-1585622764.

- WHO Report on the global tobacco epidemic, 2008 (foreword and summary). World Health Organization. 2008. pp. 8. "Tobacco is the single most preventable cause of death in the world today."

- Heckewelder, History, Manners and Customs of the Indian Nations who Once Inhabited Pennsylvania, p. 149 ff.

- Women and the Tobacco Epidemic: Challenges for the 21st Century 2001, pp.5-6.

- Surgeon General's Report - Women and Smoking 2001, p.47.

- "WHO/WPRO-Tobacco". World Health Organization Regional Office for the Western Pacific. 2005.

Coming Soon From Christopher A. Sachs

The National Registry of Haunted Places Ghost Hunter Guide

The Book of Stuff: A Parody of Life

The Long Road Home, A Novel

World War II: Attack on America, A Novel

Tales From the Dark Side: The EMS Chronicles

About the Author

Chris lives with his wife and daughter in Blacksburg, VA. He is a "plank owner" or founding member of the US Department of Homeland Security. When he isn't "saving lives" as a member of the Emergency Services, he works on a number of other books he is writing.

www.ingramcontent.com/pod-product-compliance
Lightning Source LLC
Chambersburg PA
CBHW062048280526
45788CB00003B/1154